Gunners for the Union

Gunners for the Union
Two Accounts of the Ohio Artillery
During the American Civil War

Our Battery; or the Journal of
Company B, 1st O. V. A.

O. P. Cutter

A Battery at Close Quarters

Henry M. Neil

LEONAUR

Gunners for the Union
Two Accounts of the Ohio Artillery During the American Civil War
Our Battery; or the Journal of Company B, 1st O.V.A.
by O. P. Cutter
and
A Battery at Close Quarters
by Henry M. Neil

First published under the titles

Our Battery; or the Journal of Company B, 1st O.V.A.
and
A Battery at Close Quarters

Leonaur is an imprint of Oakpast Ltd

Copyright in this form © 2011 Oakpast Ltd

ISBN: 978-0-85706-701-2 (hardcover)
ISBN:978-0-85706-702-9 (softcover)

http://www.leonaur.com

Publisher's Notes

Contents

Our Battery; or the Journal of Company B, 1st O.V. A

O. P. Cutter

Contents

DEDICATION.
TO COLONEL JAMES BARNETT,
COMMANDING THE FIRST OHIO ARTILLERY,
THAN WHOM A BRAVER,
OR KINDER HEARTED MAN TO THE SOLDIER
DOES NOT EXIST,
THIS HUMBLE WORK IS RESPECTFULLY INSCRIBED
BY HIS FRIEND,

The Author

Author's Note.—This little work was hastily written during the leisures of Camp Life, and without any intention of ever putting it in print. But, by the urgent entreaties of his companions-in-arms, the author has finally concluded to risk it—incomplete though it be—in the hands of a generous public.

CHAPTER 1

We Depart

In accordance with the proclamation of President Lincoln, calling out troops for three years, or during the war—which in future history will be better known as the great Southern Rebellion—a regiment of light artillery was at once organized in this state, and the command given to Col. James Barnett, of Cleveland, than whom no person was more qualified for the position. For many years previous to the present outbreak he had interested himself in the study of artillery, and for some time commanded a battery in this city, which, under his skilful management, became highly proficient.

Of the batteries composing the above regiment, Co. B, of which we are about to give the journal, was the second organized, and W. E. Standart elected Captain, and J. A. Bennett and J. H. Sypher as First Lieutenants, and N. A. Baldwin and E. P. Sturges for Second Lieutenants. All the commissioned officers and a portion of the non-commissioned and privates, were residents of Cleveland or its vicinity.

On Thursday, September 4th, 1861, the company having been recruited to the maximum number, we took our departure from Cleveland. A large number of relatives and friends had assembled at the depot to see us off. At 2.40 p. m., the train on which we embarked moved slowly out of the depot amid the cheers of the people. At Grafton, Wellington, and other points along the road, we were joined by a large number of recruits, who had enlisted in these and surrounding towns. Many of their friends and relatives were present to bid the bold "soger boys" goodbye. Early the same evening we arrived at Columbus, were delayed for an hour, then got under way, and reached Camp Dennison the following morning, when we at once formed in line and marched to our quarters.

At Camp Dennison commenced our first experience of a soldier's life. We were quartered in shanties built for the purpose, eight or ten persons to each. The first day was passed in looking around the camp. The next, we had guard mounting, and were given the order of the day. Each day we were twice drilled, and soon became quite proficient in handling the guns.

A few days after arriving at camp we were regularly mustered into the United States' service, when we received our clothing and equipments, and now pitched our tents for the first time, in a beautiful grove about one mile from our old quarters. The horses, harness, and other necessary articles soon arrived, and on the 5th of October orders were received to hold ourselves in readiness to march at an hours' notice. Each member of the battery was assigned his position, and all was got in readiness to march.

On Sunday morning following, the order was given to strike tents, harness horses, and be prepared to march without delay; and, although it was then raining heavily, no time was lost. Everyone was actively engaged in getting ready. Soon came word to move, but some of our horses were inclined to disobey orders, as they refused to proceed. Camp life had not been without its charms to them; they had no inclination to give up "going to grass," so soon; but, after considerable coaxing, and a little "persuasive force," we were finally on the road, and with but little adventure, aside from our horses being once or twice stalled in the mud, we reached Cincinnati.

On arriving at the "Queen City," we were quartered at the Elm street barracks. The building is quite extensive, and built of brick. It was formerly used as an orphan asylum, and was thus rather suggestive to us poor soldiers. How many of our little band of warm hearts would ever again sit in the sunshine of home? How many of the loved and true would look

For the brave men who'd come never again,
To hearths that are broken, to hearts that are lone.

None could know the ending.

Quartered in the same building was Kinney's battery of our own regiment. We remained here but two days, during which we were visited by a large number of citizens, and by them shown much attention.

On the morning of October 8th, we were on the march to Kentucky, and crossed the Ohio River. Arriving at Covington we at once commenced getting our horses and guns on board the cars, after which we were formed in line and marched to the market house, where we partook of a good dinner that had been provided for us by the loyal and patriotic ladies and gentlemen of Covington. When we had eaten to our hearts' content, our haversacks were abundantly filled by fair hands; then, giving nine rousing cheers for Covington's noble sons and daughters, we reformed in line and marched back to the depot.

In a short time all were on board the cars and under way. We passed through Cynthiana and several small towns and arrived at Lexington, where we remained until daylight. The cars containing the horses were sent forward to Nicholsville, the drivers going with them. Those who remained at Lexington were marched up to one of the hotels and treated to a good breakfast. During the forenoon the entire train reached Nicholasville, our guns and equipments were landed, and in a short time we were once more on the march.

Early the following morning we arrived at Camp Dick Robinson, having marched sixteen miles over a good turnpike road, and through what is called "the blue grass regions." This part of the country is said to be the finest in Kentucky. We pitched our tents in an extensive field, and found quite a large body of troops who had preceded us, numbering about six thousand. The place is poorly adapted for a camping ground, wood and water being quite unhandy.

We were obliged to go three miles to the Kentucky River to water our horses. After remaining here eight days, during a portion of which time it rained, on the night of October 18th we received orders to be ready to march early the next morning.

CHAPTER 2

Battle of Wild Cat

Early the following morning, in accordance with orders, all were actively engaged in making preparations to march; and, from certain indications, it was evident that we were shortly to be called on to take part in our first battle. It had been reported that the rebels, under Gen. Zollicoffer, were advancing from Cumberland Gap to attack the Union force stationed at Camp Wild Cat. The men were all in high spirits at the prospect of soon meeting the enemy in battle array. At an early hour we were on the march, being accompanied by the Fourteenth Ohio Volunteer Infantry, under command of Col. Steedman.

At noon, we passed through the pretty little town of Lancaster. The citizens are nearly all Unionists, and they greeted us kindly as we passed along. A number of ladies brought out such provisions as they had ready cooked, and gave to us freely. At sundown, we arrived at Crab Orchard, having marched twenty miles during the day. We here camped for the night, it raining heavily at the time.

Next morning, after a hasty breakfast, were again on the tramp. After passing Crab Orchard we left the beaten turnpike over which we had for some time been travelling; and now commenced the worst trial we had yet undergone. Over rocks, into ruts, through mud, onward we went; when, about ten o'clock, reports reached us that the enemy had already commenced the attack on the First Kentucky Infantry stationed at Wild Cat, and which was yet some twenty miles distant. We therefore hurried along as speedily as the rough nature of the ground would admit, and, at four o'clock, halted at a small creek and were ordered to feed our horses and prepare supper with all possible dispatch, to be ready for an all night march. Instantly, all was activity. Ammunition chests were overhauled, and things got in readiness for the coming battle.

At dark the word "forward" was given, and away we went over hills, through valleys, and through the interminable mud. Such roads! The one leading to "Jordan" can hardly be more difficult of passage. The moon, however, was shining brightly and all night long we held our toilsome way. No word of complaint, not a murmur was heard, but with a silence only broken by the heavy tread of our horses, and the creaking and rattling of the caissons and gun carriages, we passed slowly forward. We were about to engage in our first battle for the country we loved; the country that gave us birth; and that was enough to quicken the blood, to rouse our nerves for the coming conflict.

At daylight we arrived at Rock Castle River, and here made a halt to feed horses and get breakfast. On the opposite side of the river lay Wild Cat Mountain, where we soon expected to meet the foe. Breakfast was soon dispatched, and on crossing the river, which was done by fording, we were met by messengers with orders to hurry forward, as the battle had already begun. Although we had a steep and rugged mountain of some three miles in height to ascend, and were much fatigued with our last night's march, the whip and spur were freely applied to our horses, and hurrying along at double quick were soon at the scene of action.

In less than ten minutes after our arrival we were in position, and at once opened on the enemy. They were rather taken by surprise, it being the first intimation they had received that there was any artillery on the ground. The fighting, up to this time, had been done by infantry and cavalry. The rebels were in a deep ravine, and so thick were the trees we were unable to obtain sight of them from our position, and were only guided by the smoke from their guns.

The Thirty-third Indiana Infantry were posted on a hill directly opposite our battery, while the Seventeenth Ohio and First Kentucky Infantry, together with a part of Woolford's Cavalry, were stationed away to our right. The Fourteenth Ohio Infantry were drawn up in line to our left. The rebels were making efforts to drive the Thirty-third Indiana from their position. Every shot from our guns told with good effect, and the battle continued at intervals during the day. About three o'clock in the afternoon the firing became quite brisk, and lasted for half an hour. At this time we rapidly threw shells into the enemy's cover, which they did not much relish, for their fire soon perceptibly diminished, and finally ceased.

All was now quiet. At dark, one section of our battery, under Lieutenant Sypher, moved over to where the Thirty-third Indiana held position. It being through the woods, and as there was no road, the guns were of necessity dragged by hand; but there were willing hearts and stout hands at the work, and it was speedily and safely effected.

About midnight the enemy endeavoured to outflank us, but in this they were foiled; for we opened on them, throwing two or three shot, when they at once fell back to their old position, and all again became quiet.

In the morning, nothing was to be seen or heard of the enemy. They had doubtless come to the sage conclusion,

That those who fly may fight again,
Which he can never do that's slain,

and so had quietly decamped. They had been badly whipped, and only wanted to be "let alone." Their force was estimated to be about seven thousand, while ours did not exceed two thousand, and five hundred actively engaged. The rebel loss could not have been less than two hundred and fifty killed and wounded. Our loss was four killed and twenty wounded. Twenty-eight of the enemy's dead were left on the field, and were buried by our soldiers. Three of their wounded fell into our hands, two of whom died the next day. Owing to the wild and rugged nature of the country, immediate pursuit was impossible, otherwise we would have "gobbled" the greater part of their force. The ground on which the battle was fought is said to have been the favourite hunting ground of Daniel Boone, the pioneer of Kentucky. It was rather a romantic place for a battle.

CHAPTER 3

On the Road Again

We remained at Camp Wild Cat until Thursday, Oct. 24th, and then took up our line of march on the track of the fleeing rebels. All along the road were evidences of their work of destruction, as, in their retreat, they destroyed bridges, fences, and even houses. Carcasses of horses, cattle and hogs, were strewn along the roadside. In many places they had felled large trees across the road to cover their retreat. We also saw several graves where they had buried their dead.

In the afternoon of the same day, we arrived at what is called Pittman's X Roads. The Richmond road here intersects the Lexington and Cumberland Gap road. The place derives its name from an old settler.

We here pitched our tents upon a pretty knoll. It was quite convenient to wood and water, and was the most pleasant place we had yet occupied.

While here, large reinforcements were received, being an entire brigade, composed of the following regiments, namely: Fourteenth, Seventeenth and Thirty-eighth Ohio; Thirty-third Indiana; First Kentucky; First and Second Tennessee; all Infantry, and a small detachment of Woolford's Cavalry, with our own and Kinney's Batteries, of the First Ohio Artillery.

While here, we had several night alarms, but none of them proved of much consequence. In each instance, however, we were promptly prepared for any emergency. A few days later, word came to strike tents and proceed on to London, some three miles distant.

We reached London about noon of the same day, and took our bivouac in a large field on the outskirts of the town. Some of the brigade arrived the night previous, having been pushed forward, from a report that the enemy were advancing on the place. This, however, proved false. But we at once took up good positions, and made preparations to resist any attack. Detachments were sent out to reconnoitre, but without discovering any signs of the rebels. They had retired to their old quarters at Cumberland Gap.

The country around London is rough and mountainous, and the people are mostly of the poorer class. They are generally loyal to the "old flag." The population of the town is about five hundred. Most of the inhabitants had fled on the approach of the rebel army, but returned to their homes on our arrival. The buildings are, for the greater part, rickety affairs. There are but few good houses in the place. The stars and stripes, which had been torn down by vandal hands, were again raised, when the people were addressed by those noble patriots, Andy Johnson and Horace Maynard, both of Tennessee.

After remaining here quietly for two weeks, we changed our camping ground, moving about a mile west of the town, the officers thinking it to be a more desirable place for the purpose. But ere the tents had been pitched, an order came to cook three days' rations, and be prepared to march early in the evening. All wondered what was up, and various were the conjectures. The most reasonable supposition was, that we were going to attack the enemy. What was our surprise, when, on forming into line, to find ourselves faced towards Wild Cat.

At last came the word to march. Regiment after regiment fell into line as we filed past, for our battery was to take the lead. Soon the entire brigade was in motion. Wild Cat was reached and passed, but forward was the order. It was now past midnight, with the moon shining brightly. Rock Castle River was crossed; and after marching some two miles further we came to a halt. In the meantime the moon had sunk beyond the western hills, and it was now quite dark. Fires were built, around which we gathered and patiently waited for daylight. Our brigade was strewn along the road for miles, and their watch-fires streamed brightly athwart the gloom, but all was quiet, save the mournful hoot of an owl perched in the neighbouring forest, and the measured tread of the sentinels as they paced their weary beat.

Daylight came at last, and with it came rain. The command was given to move on, and forward we went, the rain pouring down in torrents, and the roads in a horrible condition. At almost every step, poor, weary, worn out soldiers sank by the road-side, being completely exhausted and unable to proceed further.

About four o'clock in the afternoon, the advance of our battery arrived at Mount Vernon. Here they halted for the remainder to come up, but finally took up quarters in a large field just in rear of the town, and it was decided upon to remain there for the night. Our guns came stringing along, and at dark all had not arrived. A small quantity of coffee was procured, from which, with some raw pork, we made the best meal we could. Fires were kindled, around which the weary souls gathered to obtain, if possible, a little sleep. Some crouched under wagons, others stowed themselves away in sheds and barns. The wagons containing our tents and mess chests were still back on the road.

Such a night as we passed through, will never be forgotten. All were wet to the skin, and many had no overcoats nor blankets.

Morning came at last, and with it a bright sun; but the air was raw and chilly. A breakfast similar to last night's supper was procured and soon eaten. After waiting some time for the rest of the battery to come up, we finally moved on without them. A march of ten miles brought us to a short distance from Crab Orchard. Here, much to our satisfaction, we were ordered to encamp. No time was lost in obeying the command, and what few tents had arrived were soon pitched. A hasty supper was cooked, and as speedily demolished. Soon, all had turned in for a night's rest, being the first we had been able to obtain for two days.

Thus ended one of the most disastrous forced marches during the war. Many a poor fellow owes his death to this cause.

The day following, the rest of the battery arrived, and we remained here until Tuesday noon, the 19th of November, when we were ordered to march, our destination being Lebanon. Alonzo Starr, of our company, died the night previous at Mount Vernon, a victim of the forced march above alluded to. His remains were sent home in charge of Corporal Blanchard. This was the first death in the battery. A number of our sick were left behind; one of whom, E. K. Bailey, died on the 17th of December. After marching about eight miles during the day, we encamped for the night, and the next morning were again on the move, marching some eighteen miles, when we halted near a small creek.

The weather up to this time had been quite pleasant, but the following morning it commenced raining, still we pushed forward, the rain continuing during the day. In the afternoon passed through the village of Caynaville, rather a small place. The same night pitched our tents in a field near a creek, about six miles from Lebanon. The weather on the next day was clear but quite cold, and we again resumed our march. During the forenoon we halted and camped on a high hill, a short distance from the town, which lay in plain view. The Fourteenth Ohio Infantry were still with us.

Four days later our right section was ordered forward to Somerset, it having been reported that a large rebel force under Zollicoffer had made an attack on the Twelfth Kentucky Infantry, Col. Hoskins, who were camped on the Cumberland River, about five miles from Somerset. According to orders, at nine o'clock in the morning, the right section, under Lieut. Bennett, started, and at noon the remainder of the battery were sent forward. Shortly after dark we came up with Bennett's command, and halted for the night. We here found the paymaster, who, the next morning, paid over our first instalment, being up to the 1st of November.

After receiving our pay, again moved forward in a heavy rain, which continued through the day, and late in the afternoon the advance reached Danville, and encamped two miles beyond the town. At dark all had arrived. Most of the men were quartered in town for the night, procuring their suppers at the hotels, and at private residences. The citizens did all in their power to make us comfortable during our short stay. A number of us obtained beds at the hotels, by paying for them, which was done willingly, for a comfortable bed we had not for a long time enjoyed.

In the morning, after passing a short time doing our trading, all returned to camp, and were again soon on the move. The right section had gone on ahead, under command of Lieutenant Baldwin—Lieutenant Bennett having received a short furlough to go home. We passed through Stanford during the day, and pitched tents four miles beyond the town. Next morning continued our march. The weather was clear, but quite cool. After marching fifteen miles, encamped near a church in progress of erection. That night the boys lodged in the church—probably the first time some of them were ever in one. Early in the morning were again moving.

Every one that we now met, reported that a battle was going on at the river just beyond Somerset. In a short time we distinctly heard cannonading, and pushed on as fast as possible, at noon arriving at Somerset. We were here informed that a regular battle was being fought at the river, five miles distant. The Seventeenth and Thirty-eighth Ohio Infantry were close on our rear, and all possible dispatch was made to reach the river, as the men were anxious to have a hand in the fun, as they called it.

At two o'clock we reached the river. It was snowing quite hard, and the firing had ceased. This was on Monday, December 2nd.

We here found Lieutenant Baldwin, and his command. It appears that the firing had all been done by the rebels, who were on the opposite side of the river. They had been throwing shot and shell into the camp of the Twelfth Kentucky, but without execution, only causing the Twelfth to move further back from the river, and out of reach of their guns.

Occasionally the rebels would march forward in regiments, fire a volley, and then fall back. Our guns made no reply, we not firing a shot. There had been some slight skirmishing between the enemy and the Twelfth Kentucky a day or two previous to our arrival. Colonel Hoskins had a small mountain howitzer, with which he now and then sent them a shell. No more firing took place that night after our arrival.

The following morning, after vainly endeavouring to make some discovery of the enemy, but seeing nothing of them, it was concluded that they had gone down the river about sixteen miles, to what is called Mill Springs, and that they would there make an attempt to cross, as at that place the river is sometimes fordable. Accordingly, Lieutenant Sypher was directed to take part of the battery and proceed to that point, to prevent their crossing. The Seventeenth Ohio Infantry had previously gone on as far as Fishing Creek, and there Lieutenant Sypher joined them. They then proceeded on towards the river, Lieutenant Sypher having the front. On enquiring of people living along the road, they were informed that none of the enemy had crossed the river; and when they had arrived to within six miles of the ford, a halt was ordered.

After some consultation, Colonel Connel, and Captain Rickards, of the Seventeenth Ohio, and Lieutenant Sypher, concluded to go forward, by themselves, and reconnoitre. When near the river, and in a deep ravine, they were suddenly fired upon by a number of Secesh Cavalry, and ordered to halt. But, instead of obeying this command, they put spurs to their horses, and made "tracks" as fast as possible, the rebels firing several volleys after them. In their flight, Colonel Connel's horse stumbled and fell, throwing the colonel off, by which means he lost his cap and sword, and was badly bruised. Captain Rickards immediately came to his assistance, and gave him his horse, the captain making his way out on foot. All got safely back to their men.

It was now evident that a large body of the enemy had already crossed, and there being no chance of obtaining a desirable position, and not having sufficient force to contend with them, they determined to fall back to Fishing Creek, and await further orders. A retreat was ordered, and our men retired in good order, and at daylight next morning were safely arrived at Fishing Creek. In the meantime, the balance of the battery were on the way to their assistance, and on the night previous were camped only two miles from the creek, where we soon found them.

We remained here through the day, and early in the evening were ordered to have all the horses harnessed, and everything ready in case of an emergency; information having been received that the enemy were advancing. One section of the battery, under Lieutenant Baldwin, was posted on the spur of a hill, commanding the crossing of the creek. A part of the Seventeenth Ohio were also stationed with them, and all were prepared for an attack.

About ten o'clock, our pickets were driven in by the enemy's advance. They reported the rebels in large force; and it being deemed folly to contend against such odds, General Schoepf, who was then in command, thought it advisable to fall back on Somerset, and there await reinforcements. We were soon retiring in good order, and before daylight arrived at Somerset. The Thirty-eighth Ohio, and Twelfth Kentucky, coming in about the same time. Shortly after daylight we moved about two miles North of the town, and encamped. This was on Thursday, December 5th.

CHAPTER 4

The Battle of Mill Springs

We remained quietly at Somerset until December 8th. In the meantime, were reinforced by the arrival of the Thirty-first and Thirty-fifth Ohio Infantry, and also Hewitt's Kentucky Battery. In addition to the above, was a small detachment of Woolford's Cavalry.

On Sunday noon, one of the cavalrymen came riding into camp in hot haste, and nearly out of breath. He stated that the enemy were advancing, and that they had made an attack on our picket guard, killing and wounding several, and had taken the rest prisoners.

At first, his story was doubted. It, however, proved true in many respects. One of the guard was killed, one wounded, and fifteen or twenty taken prisoners, all of them belonging to the Thirty-fifth Ohio. Immediately, bustle and confusion pervaded the camp. The long roll was beaten in the infantry, and all were soon in line for action. Our horses were harnessed, tents struck, when we at once proceeded towards Somerset, which we had only left a few hours previous; and, at double quick, soon went rushing into the town.

We at once took up position on a high hill just north of the town, which gave us a fine command of the country. The Seventeenth Ohio were stationed with us. The remainder of the force were stationed at different points, and all quietly awaited an attack; but at dark, no enemy had appeared. The horses were kept harnessed, and every one remained near his post of duty all night.

During the night, we were reinforced by the arrival from London of the First and Second Tennessee Infantry. The next morning nothing was seen or heard of the enemy, and it was supposed that they had become alarmed during the night, and had fallen back to their intrenchments at Mill Springs. Small reconnoitring parties were sent out daily, but with the exception of a few slight skirmishes, and occasionally a little firing between the picket guards, nothing of importance occurred for a number of days. During these skirmishes, a few prisoners were taken on both sides, so that neither derived but little advantage. The weather for about two weeks, continued fine; but neither force seemed inclined to make good use of it.

On the 17th December, Gen. Schoepf ordered the whole brigade to be in readiness to make a reconnoisance the next day. That night, one day's provisions were cooked, and all prepared for an early start. At daylight, December 18th, the entire brigade, with the exception of a sufficient number of men to guard the camp, were on the move. The forces were divided into two divisions. The Ohio and Kentucky Regiments, with two sections of our battery, under General Schoepf, went up Fishing Creek. The two Tennessee Regiments, with the right section of our battery, under Lieutenant Bennett, General Carter commanding, went down the creek.

The division of General Schoepf did not effect anything, being unable to fall in with the enemy. General Carter's command, however, was more successful. They came upon a party of the rebel cavalry, who were on the opposite side of the creek, and being out of rifle distance, they were inclined to be quite bold and defiant. But Lieutenant Bennett got his guns in position, and sent over several shells, which caused them to "skedaddle" in all directions. It was supposed that his shot killed and wounded several, as they were seen carrying off a number. They left considerable plunder which fell into the hands of the Tennessee men.

Seeing no further prospect of drawing out the enemy, the expedition returned to Somerset, arriving at dark.

Nothing of further importance occurred for some time, with the exception of an attempt on the part of Colonel Hoskins, with his regiment, and a part of the Thirty-eighth Ohio, to capture a forage train of the enemy, but which proved unsuccessful. The weather had now become cold and rainy, making the roads almost impassable; and, it was thought that nothing would be done before Spring, as neither party seemed inclined to throw down the gauntlet. But things were quietly working, and which the following will show was to some purpose.

On Friday morning, January 17th, 1862, in accordance with orders of the previous evening, the entire available force then at Somerset, set out, as was then supposed, for another reconnoisance, towards the enemy's lines. Subsequent events showed that it resulted far different from what most of the men anticipated. All camp equipage was left behind, in charge of a sufficient guard. At an early hour a start was effected; but, owing to the bad condition of the roads, slow progress was made. The late rains had swollen Fishing Creek, so that it was almost impassable; and it was at a late hour of the night ere the Battery succeeded in crossing the stream.

It now commenced raining quite hard, but the men bravely pushed forward, and, near midnight, arrived at the camp of General Thomas, who had a large force under his command. They had come over the Columbia road. This was quite a surprise to all, except such officers as were in the secret.

It now became evident that an exciting time was at hand, and that a battle was soon to be fought. But little did we soldiers dream that it would result so gloriously to our cause as the sequel will show. The rain kept pouring down, and all were wet to the skin, having no tents to protect us. At daylight next morning, it was still raining. A consultation was held between Generals Thomas and Schoepf, the result of which was known only to themselves. A part of Schoepf's Brigade was ordered back to Somerset, to act as a reserve. Our battery, with the two Tennessee regiments, remaining. Teams were sent to Somerset for provisions, with which they were loaded, and sent forward.

The rain, which had fallen heavily during the entire day, had swollen the creek to such a height that they were not able to recross until the following morning.

All of Saturday the men remained in camp, on account of the rain. The various regiments were scattered over a large extent of ground. On Sunday, January 19th, at an early hour, a part of Woolford's Cavalry, who were on picket guard, were driven in by the advance of the enemy, and soon thereafter the attack was commenced on the Tenth Indiana Infantry, who were camped in an advanced position. The Tenth stood their ground manfully for a long time, although they were opposed by four times their number. At length the Fourth Kentucky came to their relief.

The engagement had now become general. For a time our guns could not be brought to bear upon the enemy, owing to the nature of the ground, and the position of our troops, without endangering our own men. After considerable manoeuvring, a portion of the guns were got into a favourable position, and soon begun to pour in a deadly fire upon the enemy. Shot and shell flew thick and fast. Each discharge wrought fearful execution, and the rebel ranks were rapidly thinned.

The fighting had now become terrific, the advantage changing alternately from one side to the other; and at times it was difficult to tell how the battle was going. Our troops fought bravely, not once flinching. Although their comrades were falling around them, still they pressed bravely forward. General Zollicoffer fell in the early part of the engagement, having been shot through the heart by Colonel Fry, of the Fourth Kentucky.

The enemy had now begun to waver, and gradually gave ground, when the gallant Ninth Ohio made a grand bayonet charge, which scattered them in all directions. The retreat then became general. Our forces followed them up, firing volley after volley into their disordered ranks. In the meantime, the guns of our battery were doing fearful execution among the fleeing rebels. Many of the shells exploded in their very midst.

We still kept up the pursuit, the rain all the time falling heavily, which rendered the roads almost impassable; but on we went, through woods, over logs and stumps, through brush and mud. At times it was all our horses could do to pull through, and our progress was consequently slow. The roads and woods were scattered with the dead and wounded of both armies. The track of the fleeing rebels was strewn with muskets, swords, knapsacks, overcoats, &c., which they had thrown away to facilitate their flight.

At about five o'clock we had succeeded in driving the enemy behind their intrenchments at Mill Springs, being a distance of eight miles from where the battle commenced. Reinforcements had now come up, and though the men were nearly exhausted, having eaten nothing since early morning, and were saturated with the rain, the guns were soon got in position, and opened with shell on the enemy's works. The rebels replied with a few ineffectual shot, their shell falling far short of their destination. Kinney's and Wetmore's Batteries were also engaging the enemy from different positions. About eight in the evening the enemy's guns were silenced, and in a short time the firing ceased altogether. An hour later quiet reigned in the camp.

Our weary men now stretched themselves on the cold, damp ground, to obtain a little repose from the toils of the day. All slept near their post of duty, and were ready to spring into action at sound of the bugle. At early dawn they were at their stations, to renew the battle; but no sound came from the enemy's camp.

It was now determined to make a grand charge, and storm the rebel works. All the forces were drawn up in line of battle, and, at the same time, our guns were got in readiness to open on the enemy. At last the word to charge was given, and with a loud yell, the brave troops rushed forward, and were soon scaling the entrenchments. But what was their surprise, when reaching the top of the breastworks, to find the place evacuated. The birds had flown; or to use their own favourite phrase, "skedaddled." They had succeeded in crossing the river in a small steamer. A shell from our battery struck the boat just as it had crossed for the last time. The shell exploded, setting the boat on fire, and it was soon burned to the water's edge.

Having no means of crossing our forces, we were unable to follow them up. They had attempted to get part of their guns over the river, but our near approach prevented them from doing so. They left several sticking fast in the mud. A large number of the rebels could yet be seen climbing the hill on the opposite side of the river, when a few shell thrown among them caused them to scatter in wild confusion. So great was their fright, and in such a hurry were they to get away, that they left everything behind, even to their half-cooked rations. They saved nothing, except what they had on their backs.

The result of this glorious victory to the Union cause, is summed up as follows: From three hundred to four hundred of the enemy killed and wounded, and two hundred taken prisoners. About fifteen hundred horses and mules, five hundred wagons and harness, fourteen guns, with *caissons* and equipments complete, five thousand muskets, together with a large quantity of provisions, clothing and ammunition, fell into our hands. But the best of all, by this victory we succeeded in freeing this part of Kentucky of the secesh army, much to the gratification of the good Union people.

This was the first, of a series of brilliant victories that soon followed. The enemy's force in this engagement, was about ten thousand; while our force, actually engaged, did not exceed three thousand five hundred—they having about three to our one. Our men got a large quantity of trophies, in the shape of guns, revolvers, watches and clothing.

The following list comprises our force engaged in the battle: Tenth Indiana, Fourth Kentucky, Ninth Ohio, Second Minnesota, part of the First Tennessee, all Infantry, and a portion of Woolford's Cavalry, together with our own and Kinney's and Wetmore's Batteries, First Ohio Artillery.

This battle has been given several names; such as, battle near Somerset, Battle of Fishing Creek, Logan's X Roads, Old Fields, and Mill Springs. It is better known by the last mentioned.

It was not until Wednesday evening, the 22nd of January, that our battery arrived in camp at Somerset, having been absent six days. Although the men were well nigh worn out, yet all were in high spirits over their late victory, and for a long time it was the only thing talked of.

CHAPTER 5

Here a Little, and There a Little

As has been stated, it was on the 22nd of January, when the battery returned to Somerset. The next day, we went back to Mill Springs with our horses, to bring away the guns captured from the enemy.

As it was late in the day, when we arrived at the scene of the engagement, and the roads being in bad condition, we remained over night. The next morning, at daylight, started on our return, and reached Somerset at 2 p. m., the distance travelled in both expeditions being sixty-four miles.

We now received orders to march for East Tennessee; but the order was soon after countermanded, as it was found impossible to proceed, owing to the horrible condition of the roads. Colonel Barnett had arrived shortly after the battle, it being the first time we had seen him since leaving Camp Dick Robinson. He remained with us only a few days.

Not having before said anything about Somerset, we will here describe the place:—It is one of the early settled towns of Kentucky, and like all the other mountain towns of this state, it presents rather a sombre and gloomy appearance. The buildings are mostly built of wood, and are old fashioned affairs. The business part looks as if it had gone through the revolutionary war; many of the buildings are fast going to decay. The population is about one thousand five hundred. Although the inhabitants profess to be loyal to the old government, yet many of them are, at heart, rank secessionists. There is a court-house and jail here, it being the seat of justice for Pulaski County.

We remained here until the 10th of February, 1862, being a period of just ten weeks from the day of our first arrival. On Saturday, the 8th of the same month, Edward C. Chapman, a member of our company, died, and was buried the next day. His remains were followed to the grave by nearly all the members of the battery. This was the first burial in the company, the others, who died, having been sent home, with the exceptions of Hodge and Bailey, who were left sick at towns we passed through.

It having been found impracticable to go forward into East Tennessee, for various reasons, on Saturday, February 8th, we were ordered to be prepared to march on the following Monday.

Monday morning found us ready to move; and, at 8 o'clock, we bade good bye to Somerset, much to our satisfaction. We marched twelve miles that day, over the worst kind of a road. In many places the mud was belly deep to the horses, and they often got stalled. At night, camped in a small valley near a creek. During the night, a heavy snow storm set in, and, in the morning, the ground was covered, and more still falling. At 8 o'clock, were again on the move. The roads were but little better than the day previous; we were, however, in a more open country. Marched this day about fourteen miles, and at 4 o'clock struck the turnpike at a small creek, where there was a mill, and one or two stores. We proceeded one mile beyond, and camped for the night—the weather cold and stormy.

Next morning, the weather was quite pleasant; and, as soon as breakfast was over, were again on the road. Lieutenant Bennett was taken sick, and was left at this place. We now had a good road, and made fair progress. At 4 o'clock, we camped two miles from Danville, the town being in plain view. The distance made this day, was twenty-four miles.

Danville is one of the most beautiful towns in Kentucky. The streets are wide and clean, and the place is well laid out. The population is about five thousand. It contains many fine buildings, both public and private.

Early next morning, as usual, on the move, with fine weather. Lieutenant Sturges was left sick with typhoid fever at Houston-ville, on our way through. Marched twenty miles this day, and camped in the woods eight miles from Lebanon. There was a heavy fall of snow during the night, and the morning was ush-ered in cold and disagreeable, but we were soon moving, and ar-rived at Lebanon about noon, and camped two miles from town on the Louisville road.

Time, on the above march, four and a half days.

At Lebanon, we received a supply of new clothing, and also our Sibley tents, which made us more comfortable. At this place, we obtained the news of the capture of Forts Henry and Donel-son. Our horses were shod, and some of them exchanged for others. Also received a lot of army wagons, with six mules to each. Had considerable sport in breaking in the mules, many a laughable incident occurring. One of them, in particular, seemed inclined to have his own way, in spite of all the driver's efforts to render him tractable. He would neither go forwards nor back-wards; and when Jehu applied whip and spurs, as an inducement to proceed, he would turn his head, look his tormentor full in the face, with a most wicked leer, and then commence such a series of "ground and lofty tumblings," that the driver was feign to hold on for dear life.

Finally, a bright idea seized the mind of our mounted friend. "Boys," said he, "I'll bet two to one, that I make this cloven-footed, tobacco-leaf-eared model of a Dutch church sweat the hide off hisself;" and, leaving his animal tied to a fence, he en-tered a grocery, soon returning with an immense cabbage stuck on the point of his sword. Once more mounting the sagacious beast, Jehu laid his sword between the animal's ears. The cabbage projecting in full view to the enraptured gaze of the refractory steed, caused him to elevate his muzzle for so tempting a morsel, and, in the attempt, he began to move forward, and soon was going at a speed wonderful to behold. That mule always went well after that. He was partial to cabbages.

We had orders to move on Tuesday, the 18th of the same

month; but, owing to the rainy weather, did not leave. From preparations being made, it looked as if we were going to have another long and tedious march. Only the officers knew our destination. The weather during our stay here, had been wet and cold.

Theodore White died in hospital on the night of February 18th. His remains were sent home in charge of his brother, who was quite sick. A large number of sick were left in hospital at this place, among whom was Corporal H. P. Fenn, who died shortly after our departure. Lieutenant Bennett returned on the 20th, having nearly recovered from his sickness.

Friday morning opened bright and clear, and we took our departure from Lebanon, having been here one week.

At 8 o'clock, were on the way, and, at 11 a. m., passed through the town of Springfield. Marched twenty-five miles that day, and pitched our tents in the woods, five miles from Bardstown. The next morning was rainy. Proceeded to within one mile of the town, and again camped. Kinney's battery accompanied us. This was the 22nd of February, being Washington's birthday. At noon, Kinney's battery fired a salute, in honour of the occasion. The next day, went about four miles beyond Bardstown and again camped in the woods. A large number of troops were camped near us.

On Monday morning, the 24th, we started for Louisville. Nearly all of Thomas' Division were with us, making quite a large army. Marched twenty-six miles this day, and camped for the night near a small village. The next morning, got an early start, and arrived within three miles of Louisville. It was now the 25th of February.

We camped in a large field near the city, and the following day were paid for two months' services, being up to the 1st of January. This was the second payment we had received.

It was now generally understood, that we were bound up the Cumberland River; but for what point, was not fully known. General Thomas' Division kept coming in, regiment after regiment; proceeded directly to the city, and there embarked aboard the steamers which were chartered for the purpose. A number of our men went into the city, after being paid.

Louisville is the largest and most important city in Kentucky. It is situated at the falls of the Ohio River, and contains a population of seventy thousand, and is the centre of a large and growing trade.

On Thursday morning, the 27th of February, we entered the city, and at once commenced getting the guns, horses, &c., on board the steamer Westmoreland. It was nearly dark, ere this was completed. At 10 o'clock the same evening, we cast loose from the levee and were soon steaming down the broad Ohio. Sixteen boats loaded with troops accompanied us. Colonel Barnett was on one of them; and there were also two or three more of his batteries on different boats.

Lieutenant Sypher, who had been absent on a short furlough, joined us at Louisville.

The late heavy rains had caused quite a freshet in the Ohio river and its tributaries. Many towns and buildings, which we passed, were almost submerged, and in some places the river spread out in lake-like expansion. We frequently met boats, which were returning for troops and supplies, having discharged their loads. Making but few stops, and only then for the purpose of "coaling," on Sunday morning, March 2nd, we arrived at Smithland, at the mouth of the Cumberland. We made but a short stay here, and then went steaming up the river.

It was now well understood, that Nashville was our destination. The Cumberland, like the Ohio, was at a high stage, and our progress against the current was but slow. About 4 o'clock in the afternoon, we arrived at Fort Donelson, and as we made but a short stop, had no opportunity to go on shore to see the place, but had a pretty good view of it as we passed by. There were a large number of Union troops stationed here, who heartily cheered us on passing. The stars and stripes were floating over the fort, where erst the hated symbol of secession flung its disgraceful folds.

On Monday morning, we passed the city of Clarksville, Tennessee, but made no landing. A band, on board one of the transports accompanying us, played several national airs as we steamed along. The place seemed almost deserted. Occasionally, a group of "woolly heads" could be seen, displaying their "ivories," and swinging their old hats. Here, as at Fort Donelson, were a large number of troops, and the good old flag was flying. The railroad bridge, over the river, had been partially destroyed by fire, when the Federal gunboats first made their appearance before the city. On Tuesday morning, March 4th, we arrived at Nashville, having been four days on the trip.

At Nashville, we found about fifty steamers discharging their loads. All of them had brought troops and munitions of war. There had already twenty thousand troops arrived, and more constantly coming. Our guns and caissons were got ashore at once, the men and horses remaining on board until next morning, when we disembarked, and took up our line of march for the camping ground, passing through several of the principal streets. We proceeded out on the Charlotteville road some three miles from the city, and pitched our tents on a beautiful spot, near a small creek. Bartlett's and Kinney's batteries were camped nearby. We had dress parade at 4 p. m. each day. The weather was very changeable, sometimes being cold, with rain and snow, at other times quite warm and pleasant.

While at this camping ground, a large number of the company visited what was called Fort Zollicoffer, or, at least, what was intended for a fort, or defence, for the protection of Nashville. It is situated on a high bluff, three miles below the city, on the Cumberland River, and consists of a slight earthwork. There were several large guns laying half buried in the mud; only two remaining mounted, the rebels having hastily attempted to destroy the works, on the approach of the Union gun-boats. Shot and shell, were laying around in large quantity.

Remaining at this camp until Sunday, March 16th, we moved our quarters two miles south of the city, on the Franklin Pike, and near the Tennessee and Alabama Railroad. We here pitched our tents, on a high ridge between the railroad and turnpike.

Colonel Barnett named it Camp Brownlow, in honour of that sterling old patriot, Parson Brownlow. There were also camped nearby, several batteries from Kentucky, Wisconsin, and other states. Colonel Barnett, had the entire command. We were kept under thorough military discipline. Dress parade every afternoon, drilling and guard mounting. After remaining here about one week, for some cause or other, we again moved half a mile to new grounds. While here, a number of the sick were discharged the service. Those who had been left sick at different points, and had recovered, here rejoined us. Richard Williams, a member of our company, died in the hospital at Nashville on the 15th of March. He was from Cleveland.

Nashville, the capital of Tennessee, is situated on the Cumberland River, two hundred and fifty miles from its mouth. It is the terminus of the Louisville and Nashville Railroad, and is also the centring point of numerous other southern roads. It is sometimes known as the City of Rocks; being built on a high rocky elevation. The population is about twenty-five thousand, and it is a place of considerable trade. Most of the cotton, and other products of Middle Tennessee, here find a market.

The State House, is a large and magnificent structure, built entirely of marble, and situated on a high elevation called Capitol Hill. It is the first object that attracts the attention of the stranger, on his approach to the city, as it can be seen from a considerable distance from all quarters of approach. The glorious old flag, under which our fathers fought in a cause most holy, now floats from its dome, in place of the late Secesh rag. The streets are narrow and irregular, not being laid out with any regard to beauty. There are a large number of fine buildings here, both public and private. The citizens are, for the most part, strong secessionists. The appearance of Union soldiers in their streets was not much relished, but they were obliged to put up with it.

On the 29th of March, we struck tents, and again moved forward, taking the Franklin road, in company with the Seventy-ninth Pennsylvania, First Wisconsin, and Thirty-fifth Indiana, all infantry, and one regiment of Pennsylvania Cavalry. We were now in the Seventh Brigade of General Buel's department, General Negley commanding. A march of twenty miles through heat and dust, brought us to the pretty little town of Franklin, and at 4 o'clock in the afternoon we camped in a grove one mile from the town. Nearly all the places of business here were closed, many of the inhabitants having fled from the wrath of the "barbarous yankees." We remained here only two days, and were then again ordered forward.

On Monday morning, April 1st, we left the place. The day was quite warm, and the roads very dusty, but we marched twenty-five during the day, and camped in the woods near a creek. The men had now a good opportunity for bathing, which most of them took advantage of. This place was rather a rough camping ground, being quite uneven and covered with rocks. The next morning, had a fine shower, which cooled the atmosphere and settled the dust. At 8 o'clock were once more moving, and soon forded a creek, the rebels having destroyed the bridge. A number of the First regiment Michigan Engineers and Mechanics, were actively engaged in rebuilding it. After proceeding about two miles, were ordered to halt, remaining in the road for two hours, then moved into a field to our left, and encamped. Next day, again started, and at noon reached Columbia, having crossed Duck River. We here camped on a high hill just back of the town.

This was April 3rd.

It was about 2 o'clock, when our tents were pitched. The ground was cleared up, and the place made quite pleasant for camping purposes. It was surrounded by a heavy growth of trees, which were beginning to leave out. We also had a commanding view of the town and surrounding country.

Columbia, the county seat of Maury, is situated on Duck River, and is fifty miles from Nashville. The Tennessee and Alabama Railroad, passes through it. Population, about three thousand. The streets are wide and clean. Among the public buildings, is a large female seminary, then closed. A majority of the people are secessionists. Shortly after our arrival, Dow Tanney, a member of the company, died. On the 7th of April, the right section of the battery, under command of Lieutenant Bennett, went to Mount Pleasant, fourteen miles from Columbia. A part of our brigade, also went with them. On the 22nd of April, we received another payment, being up to March 1st. On the night of May 1st, about 11 o'clock, an order came for one section of the battery to proceed at once to Pulaski. At 12 o'clock the centre section, under Lieutenant Baldwin, started, with four companies of the Seventh Pennsylvania Cavalry, one company First Kentucky, and four companies Seventy-ninth Pennsylvania Infantry, accompanying.

The reason of this sudden movement, was on account of Morgan's cut-throat cavalry being at Pulaski, where they had captured a wagon train of General Mitchell's division, and had also made an attack on a party of unarmed Union soldiers, who had just been discharged from hospital, and were on the way to join their regiments. A number were killed and wounded, and several taken prisoners. The citizens of Pulaski had assisted Morgan in this attack, firing on our soldiers from their houses, and had also broken open the store of a Union man, and carried off all his goods and money.

Our men pushed on as fast as possible, and, when within ten miles of the town, were met by a number of the troops, who had been captured by the enemy, and released on parole. They reported Morgan and his gang still at Pulaski, when they left. Lieutenant Baldwin having the front, gave the order to forward on double quick. The men were not slow in obeying; and at 2 o'clock went rushing into Pulaski in hot haste, but were a little too late for the rebels, as they had taken the alarm and "skedaddled."

The men retaliated on the citizens for their base conduct. They took possession of the town, and went into the mercantile business. From soldiers, they were soon turned into merchants, and opened stores on their own account. Soon all were loaded with watches, jewellery, boots, shoes, hats, clothing, etc., besides a certain other article which we wouldn't mention by a jug-full.

They remained here a few days—long enough to regulate matters, and to give the residents to understand, that they must behave themselves. For Union boys won't be trifled with.

On the 6th instant, they returned to Columbia, where they safely arrived.

On the evening of the 2nd of May we were all aroused by an order to harness horses, and every man to be at his post with all possible dispatch.

This sudden move rather took us by surprise, and all wondered what was in the wind.

It would appear that a large number of Morgan's guerrillas had been prowling in the vicinity of Columbia, and it was supposed that they intended to take advantage of the absence of part of our force, to attack the place. But it was not long ere we were in readiness to give them a warm reception. Our remaining two guns were posted on a hill a short distance from the camp, and the balance of the troops, then here, were placed in favourable positions. The night passed without any disturbance.

Morgan and his hellish crew
Were afraid to come in view.

But for several nights we maintained a strict watch for the murderous thieves.

On the morning of the 6th of May, the forge wagon was sent to Mount Pleasant, to shoe the horses of Lieutenant Bennett's section. Lieut. B. and his command were camped in a fine grove, near a large creek. The First Wisconsin and Thirty-fifth Indiana Infantry, together with some Kentucky Cavalry, were camped nearby.

On the 10th of May, an order came for them to proceed directly to Pulaski; and at noon they were on the road,—the First Wisconsin going with them. The left section had, also, an order to go to the same place, and left immediately, under command of Lieutenants Sypher and Sturges. I will here state, that Lieutenant Sypher had returned, and joined us at Columbia, some two weeks previous, having recovered his health. He had been sick nearly two months, and went home from Houstonville, where we had left him. A number of our sick, who had been left behind, rejoined us here.

On the 20th of May, Lieutenant Bennett returned to Columbia with the right section, and immediately proceeded to Kalioke Station, six miles from Columbia, and on the railroad. On the 21st inst., the left section, under Lieutenant Sypher, returned, and went into camp at the old place. The night of June 2nd, had another alarm, caused by the firing of our pickets. The next day, a Union meeting was held at the place; and during the afternoon had still another alarm, but, like the former, proved without cause. On the 29th of May, the left section again left Columbia, the centre section now only remaining; and, on the 9th of June, they also left for Murfreesboro.

CHAPTER 6

Expedition of the Centre Section

On Monday, June 9th, the centre section left Columbia for Murfreesboro, leaving the forge, battery and baggage wagons behind, together with the tents and camp equipage. The reason for this move was supposed to be an attack apprehended on Murfreesboro, as there had been several skirmishes in that vicinity.

At 5 a. m. the two guns started, under command of Captain Standart and Lieutenant Baldwin. At 2 p. m. the forge and battery wagons, together with what men were left; also left along with the First Kentucky Cavalry. Standart's command marched four miles beyond Franklin that day, and camped for the night. The remainder went within five miles of the above place, and also camped. The next day, the last-named went to within seven miles of Murfreesboro. The centre section reached the town at 2 p. m. the same day. The roads, with the exception of some six miles, were in fine order, being macadamized. The country is well adapted for farming, and we passed many large fields of wheat, corn and cotton. The wheat, generally, was being cut.

On Wednesday morning, June 11th, with our two guns we set out, in company with the Sixty-ninth and Seventy-fourth Ohio, Third Minnesota, Eleventh and part of the Ninth Michigan—all Infantry—and one battalion each of the Fourth Kentucky and Seventh Pennsylvania Cavalry, together with four guns of the First Tennessee and four of First Kentucky Artillery. At 9 o'clock, same morning, the First Kentucky Cavalry, together with our forge and battery wagon, arrived at Murfreesboro, and were at once sent forward to join the main body of the army. The expedition was under command of General Dumont.

Early that evening our expedition reached Readyville, and camped in a corn-field near a creek. At 11 o'clock, the same night, all hands were ordered out to proceed on the march. A good deal of grumbling was caused at this unlooked for command, but all must obey.

About this time, an eclipse of the moon occurred, and the men jocosely remarked that we were only wakened to take an astronomical survey of it.

After considerable delay, at 1 o'clock we were in motion. For the first few miles the road was quite hilly, and one of the Kentucky battery's *caissons* was capsized over a bank, and had to be left behind. The roads were now in pretty good condition, but very dusty, and at daylight we had advanced some ten miles. The weather was extremely warm, but the road was well shaded by woods. At 11 o'clock arrived at McMinnville, a small town of some five hundred inhabitants, and situated on the Manchester and McMinnville Railroad. The place is strongly "secesh." There was an M. D. along with us, who had lately been driven out of the town on account of strong Union sentiments. He was acting as our guide.

At McMinnville we camped in an open field near the town—the Tennessee and Kentucky Batteries being camped nearby. The remainder of the force were camped at different places. On the day following, a part of the force, consisting of the Third Minnesota, and First Kentucky Infantry, one battalion each of the Fourth Kentucky and Seventh Pennsylvania Cavalry, one section of Hewitt's Kentucky, and our centre section of artillery, were ordered forward to Pikeville, to drive out a body of Secesh Cavalry, who were reported as being at that place. At 5 p. m., took up our line of march. The next morning, early, the rest of the force followed.

Our road now lay through a wild, rough, and mountainous country, but thinly inhabited and little cultivated—corn being the only grain we saw. The long and dry continuance of the weather had drained all the creeks, so that water was not readily obtained, and, for the want of which, both man and beast suffered terribly. The hills were steep and rocky, and our poor horses, overcome with heat and thirst, were bleeding at the nose, and ready to give out; but by dint of hard urging, and easing them of their loads, we finally reached Pikeville early in the afternoon of Saturday, June 14th. Much to our disappointment, found that the secesh had left three days prior to our arrival.

Pikeville is a small place, containing one hundred and fifty inhabitants, and is situated at the head of Sequatchie Valley. It is on or near the dividing line of East and Middle Tennessee. There were several Union men living here, some of whom joined Woolford's Cavalry.

The advance, finding their mission at an end, set out on their return the next day. In the meantime the rear detachment, which had camped half way between McMinnville and Pikeville the night before, the next morning proceeded on; but when they had gone four or five miles, were ordered to face about and retrace their steps.

A day and night's march again brought us to McMinnville, where we camped on the river's bank. Those who went forward also arrived on the afternoon of the same day, which was Monday, June 16th.

We remained here until 5 o'clock on the afternoon of the 17th, and then once more moved towards Murfreesboro. Marched all night, and at daylight of the 18th entered the town of Woodbury, where we camped near our former ground. Remained here during the day, and at night resumed our march. During the night were visited by a heavy thunder storm, rendering it so dark as to be almost impossible to keep the road. At 4 o'clock next morning reached Murfreesboro, and went into camp.

Murfreesboro is quite a pretty place, and contains a population of five thousand. It is the county seat of Rutland, and is located on the Nashville and Chattanooga Railroad, being some thirty miles from the former place.

Friday morning, at daylight, we started for Columbia, free from infantry and cavalry, with the exception of one company of the First Kentucky. Captain Standart left us at Murfreesboro and went to Shelbyville, where Lieutenant Sypher was stationed with the left section. We were accordingly under command of Lieutenant Baldwin. We camped the first night, two miles beyond Franklin. Made an early start on Saturday morning, June 21st, and reached Columbia at 11 a. m. the same day. Camped on the east side of Duck River, where we found Lieutenant Bennett with the second detachment of the right section, they having arrived the night previous from Rogersville, Alabama, where they left the first detachment.

The Seventy-eighth Pennsylvania Infantry were encamped with them. All were glad to once more get back to their old quarters. We had been gone just thirteen days, during which time we had marched two hundred and fifty miles, and which resulted in no particular advantage; but, on the contrary, had considerably worn down the men and horses, besides losing our tents and part of our baggage. Take it all in all, it was the most severe march we had yet endured. Our present camping ground was not near as pleasant as formerly.

July 1st, moved our quarters one mile north-east of the town. This was a much better location in many respects. The Seventy-eighth Pennsylvania camped near us. July 4th, at 3 a. m., one section of our battery went into town, and fired a salute of thirty-four guns. At noon, the entire battery did the same. On July 9th, the left and centre sections started for Shelbyville, marching till about 8 o'clock that evening, and then halted near a creek to feed horses and get supper.

At 11 o'clock, the moon having risen, were ordered forward, and soon passed through the small town of Farmington. The stars and stripes were flying from a high staff in the centre of the town, and several of the inhabitants displayed small United States flags in front of their houses.

We were here joined by the Seventh Pennsylvania Cavalry; and, on the morning of July 10th, entered Shelbyville, where we found Lieutenant Sypher with the left section, camped one mile from town. This was the first time that the entire battery had camped together since the 7th of April. Distance from Columbia, forty miles.

Shelbyville is located on Duck River, and is the terminus of a branch of the Nashville and Chattanooga Railroad, and distant about seventy-five miles from Nashville. It contains a population of three thousand five hundred, and is the county seat of Bedford. About one-half of the residents are good Unionists.

We remained here only a few hours, being ordered off at 6 o'clock the same evening. The left section had been here nearly a month. A short time after getting under way, it commenced raining quite hard. At 10 o'clock the same night arrived at Wartrace, where we remained until next morning. We laid out in the storm all night, and, in the morning, after breakfast, went one mile from town and camped. The Seventy-ninth Pennsylvania Infantry were already here.

Wartrace is a small station on the Nashville and Chattanooga Railroad. Population about two hundred. Our camping ground was on a hill, and near a fine creek. For two days, everything was quiet; but, on Sunday morning, July 13th, at daylight, heavy firing was heard in the direction of Murfreesboro, which is about twenty miles distant. All sorts of conjectures were formed in regard to the cause of it. At night, received a report that the rebels had attacked Murfreesboro, and had succeeded in obtaining possession of the town. Had captured the Third Minnesota Infantry, and part of Hewitt's First Kentucky Battery. At first, this report was doubted, but in the end proved true.

From certain rumours current in camp, it was supposed that a force of the enemy were in the vicinity of Wartrace, and an attack was apprehended at any moment. At dark struck our tents, harnessed our horses, and made all preparation to meet the enemy. About 10 o'clock, received an order to move. The right section remained near camp. The left section took position at the depot, the centre section going out some distance below the depot, and close to the track. All kept vigilant watch during the night, but no enemy appeared.

The following day we received reinforcements, consisting of the Fifty-first Ohio, part of the Ninth Michigan, and two companies of the Third Minnesota, who were engaged in guarding some station at the time of the capture of Murfreesboro, and had luckily escaped. We also had a small force of cavalry. During the day of Monday, July 14th, scouts were sent out in different directions. A small barricade was built at the point where the centre section was posted. At night, troops were stationed in different places along the road, and the utmost caution observed to prevent a surprise. But the night passed, like the one previous, without an attack.

At daylight, the whole force was ordered to move, and were soon under way. We were not allowed to wait for breakfast, or to feed the horses. What this movement was for, or where we were going, none, save the officers in command, knew.

A march of twenty miles brought us to Tullahoma, which is south of Wartrace, and on the same railroad. It is also at the junction of the Manchester and McMinnville road. On arriving there, we encamped in an orchard near the depot. At dark, the left section were posted on a high elevation, at the north-east part of the town. There was already a large force here, and more troops still arriving. The concentrating of so large a force at this point, looked as if a battle was brewing. Preparations were at once made to resist any force the enemy might bring to oppose us. Rifle pits were dug, and earth works thrown up. Various rumours circulated through camp. Several persons were arrested on the charge of being spies; one of whom, rumour had it, was found guilty, and sentenced to be hung.

Three days thus passed by, during which time we were visited by frequent showers of rain.

On the night of the 18th of July, the centre section moved to a grove close by the depot, while the right section moved in another direction, and near where the left was posted. At 9 o'clock next morning, received orders to march, and a general breaking up of camp now took place; some going in one direction—some in another. Our battery, together with the Eighteenth Kentucky Infantry, went towards Shelbyville. Marched about nine miles that day, and camped in a large field. During the night, had a heavy thunder storm, with high wind. At daylight, were on the move. The weather was quite cloudy, and threatened more rain, but soon cleared up and became quite pleasant. At 10 o'clock a. m., entered Shelbyville, and, after remaining there an hour, again moved forward.

We were now travelling over a macadamized road, which was in most excellent condition. After going eight miles, we camped near a creek, and remained here until daylight the next morning, when we again resumed our march. At 11 o'clock a. m., arrived at Murfreesboro, where we found a large Union force, under Major General Nelson. We camped on the Nashville pike, about one mile from town. The next morning, there was quite a movement of troops. A large force headed by General Nelson went towards Nashville. Our battery moved camp to a high elevation overlooking the town. About three hundred slaves had been brought in from the surrounding country, and set to work building a redoubt for the use of artillery. Our men were engaged in putting the camping ground in good order. In a short time, report reached us that a large force of rebels had entered Lebanon and captured the place without firing a gun.

All kinds of rumours were put in circulation regarding this movement. At 4 o'clock, we received orders to harness horses and be prepared to march at any moment. About the same time, a "cock and bull" story was started, that a party of "secesh" had entered town with a flag of truce and demanded the surrender of the place. But it afterwards appeared that a small body of rebels had approached the place for the purpose of effecting an exchange of prisoners. At dark, no order had been given to move. Another sensation was created, to the effect that some rebel cavalry had been seen skulking in the upper edge of a cornfield, near which we were encamped.

All this time we were momentarily expecting to move; but, for some reason, the order was delayed. It seemed as if those in command did not know what to do. After waiting until after midnight, we at last received word to march. The night was very dark, and the clouds threatened an instant storm. We moved on at a snail-like pace until daylight, and shortly after arrived at Stone River, which we were obliged to ford, the bridge having been destroyed. We now knew that we were going towards Lebanon. The slaves along the road reported that a large body of rebel cavalry had gone towards Murfreesboro late the day previous. Here, again, was a fine opportunity to manufacture long "yarns;" and mole-hills were magnified into mountains.

Notwithstanding all this, we kept on towards Lebanon. When we had proceeded to within ten miles of the town, a halt was ordered, and some of the cavalry were sent forward to reconnoitre. In about an hour they returned, bringing in two prisoners whom they had captured. They reported that the enemy had left Lebanon. Order was now given to "about face," and we were soon on the return to Murfreesboro. When we had arrived to within two miles of where the Nashville and McMinnville road crosses the Murfreesboro and Lebanon road, it was reported that a body of the enemy were there, waiting to offer us battle; and, from the stories we had heard in the morning, it looked somewhat reasonable.

Our forces were soon drawn up in line of battle, and moved forward to meet the supposed enemy; Colonel Barnes, of the Eighth Kentucky, acting as Brigadier General.

After deploying right and left, and sending out scouts, it was soon ascertained that there was no enemy lying in wait. It was now nearly dark, and we had eaten nothing during the day, except a little hard bread and cold bacon, but the word "forward" was given, and on we went. About 7 o'clock we again crossed Stone River, and here camped, or rather bivouacked, for the night. After feeding our teams, and preparing some coffee, stretched ourselves on the ground to obtain a little sleep, being pretty well tired out.

The next morning, as soon as it was light enough to see, and without having anything to eat, we again moved forward towards Murfreesboro. We had barely gone two miles when we were ordered to about face and march back. What this all meant was more than we were able to surmise. The boys remarked that we were going back to water, and which has since been a by-word, whenever a counter-march has taken place.

Once more we crossed the river, and on arriving at the cross-roads before mentioned, were ordered to camp, which we were glad to do, though it was far from being a pleasant place. This was on the 24th of July.

We remained here until the afternoon of the 25th, without anything worthy of note transpiring. At 6 o'clock p. m. we started for Murfreesboro, arriving there at 8 o'clock the same evening. We halted in front of the court-house, and after standing some two hours, were ordered to unhitch horses, but not to take off harness, and lay by for the night. We spread our blankets on the sidewalk, and, with an excellent brick sidewalk for a bed, dreamed the hours away. Early in the morning, went to our old camping ground on the hill. This was on the 27th of July.

> Note.—The enemy which we expected to meet at the cross-roads near Stone River, on the night of the 23rd of July, proved to be General Nelson's command, who had returned by this road. Colonel Barnes—who, it will be recollected, was in command of our force—was unaware of this movement. The slaves had mistaken General Nelson's force for a body of "secesh."

CHAPTER 7

Moving—Still Moving

On arriving at the old quarters, we found the negroes still at work on the redoubt, which they had nearly completed. The Twenty-third Kentucky were camped near us. We now supposed that we would be allowed at least a short respite after our previous three weeks' hard marching; but in this we were mistaken. And, as the old Scotch proverb runs—

The best laid plans of men and mice
Oft gang aglee.

At noon of the 28th July, we received orders, (those eternal orders,) to prepare for a march at 3 o'clock that afternoon. The battery wagon, tents, and all the extra baggage, were to be left behind. At the appointed hour all was in readiness, and in a short time we were on the move. We had proceeded but a short distance when we were ordered back, and the old by-word came again in play, that we were only going to water our horses. Back to camp we went. It seemed as if those in command were diverting themselves at our expense. The next day we were permitted to remain in quiet. But at 2 o'clock on the morning of the 30th July, we were all aroused out of a sound sleep with the old oft-repeated order to get ready to march. Soon all were actively engaged in preparing to move. At daylight, after drinking a cup of slops—denominated coffee—and devouring some mouldy hard bread, we patiently awaited the order to march.

It had now commenced raining, and in a short time was

pouring down heavily. No word came to move. And thus we stood, hour after hour, and received a thorough drenching. Finally, about noon, were ordered to unharness horses, but to hold ourselves in readiness to move at any moment. Here was a piece of great military strategy displayed.

Finally, on the morning of August 1st, we succeeded in making a start. At 5 o'clock were on the road leading to McMinnville, over which a part of our battery had before travelled. The forces with us consisted of the Eighth and Twenty-first Kentucky and Fifty-first Ohio Infantry, together with a part of the Fifth Kentucky Cavalry. General Nelson headed the column. A much larger force had preceded us a few days previous. It was rumoured that there was a large force of the enemy at McMinnville, and the object of the present expedition was to drive them out. Their number was variously estimated from five thousand to forty thousand. We marched the first day as far as Woodbury, a distance of twenty miles, and camped for the night near one of our old quarters.

Early next morning, as usual, again on the move. Another "cock and bull" story was going the rounds, but little heed was given it. At 6 p. m. of the second day, August 2nd, we entered McMinnville, but instead of finding a large rebel force, we found only the residents. As near as could be ascertained, there had been some three hundred rebel cavalry in the place, who had said "goodbye" on our approach.

We pitched tents near our former camping ground. The next day, which was Sunday, we were allowed to rest. It was said that the rebels, some eight thousand or ten thousand strong, were camped nine miles distant, on the Sparta road. Our force numbered about twelve thousand. At dark, that night, received orders to be ready to march at 4 o'clock the following morning. We were further ordered not to take any extra clothing—not even our overcoats, nor cooking utensils, and but one blanket to two men.

From these orders, and what had been reported of the enemy, a fight was certainly expected. On Monday morning, at the break of day, all were ready, and soon regiment after regiment fell in line. At 5 o'clock, moved out on the Sparta road. But for some reason, unknown to us soldiers, our battery, and the Thirty-fifth Indiana Infantry, were ordered to remain in camp.

For the two succeeding days, nothing of consequence transpired. At the end of this time the expedition returned, having been unable to meet with the enemy, and therefore but little of importance was effected by this movement.

On the morning of August 6th, we moved our camp one-half mile out on the Sparta road. We were now assigned to the Twenty-third Brigade—Colonel Stanley Mathews, of the Fifty-first Ohio, acting Brigadier General. The brigade consisted of the Fifty-first Ohio, Eighth and Twenty-first Kentucky, and Thirty-fifth Indiana Infantry, together with our battery. On the 6th instant, being the same day of our removal, seven of our men, with three six-mule teams, were captured by a party of Secesh Cavalry a few miles from McMinnville, and on the Chattanooga road. They were, at the time, out foraging.

Thirteen out of fifteen of the Thirty-fifth Indiana, who went out as guards, were also captured, although they made a strong resistance. The day previous, Lieutenant Sturges and Sergeant Lewellen had been out to this place, and had made arrangements to take a lot of corn on the day following, being the one on which the men were taken prisoners. The rebels were either informed by the owners of the grain, or had got notice of it in some manner, and were lying in wait for our men. The consequence was, the men were entirely surrounded and taken by surprise. Those belonging to the battery were without arms, or any means of defence. It is said that two or three of the rebels were killed or wounded, but it lacks confirmation.

The rebels immediately hurried the men off on double quick, and, after taking them some twenty-five miles, released them on parole, leaving them to find their way back to camp on foot. They returned safe on the morning of the 8th. Shortly after their arrival, they were arrested and put in the guard house, by order of General Nelson, but for what reason was not known at the time. Subsequent events went to show that they had purposely surrendered themselves to the enemy, or had not exercised due caution in preventing surprise.

On investigation they were all honourably discharged, as none of the charges could be substantiated; but, on the contrary, it was proven that they had done all in their power to prevent being taken, and only surrendered when they became aware that any further resistance was useless. They were again ordered on duty, as those who had paroled them had acted without proper authority, and therefore it was null and void.

On Sunday, August 10th, about noon, were ordered to be ready to march at 4 o'clock, but shortly before the appointed time the order was countermanded. The next morning at daylight, got the order to "forward," and were soon in motion. One of the guns was left behind, as there were not sufficient men to handle it. The Eighth and Twenty-first Kentucky, and Fifty-first Ohio, with a small detachment of the Fifth Kentucky Cavalry, and our battery, constituted the force, all under the command of Brigadier General Jackson. A march of eighteen miles brought us to the town of Smithville, and about 4 o'clock we camped a short distance beyond the place.

We here found the Thirty-first Indiana and Twenty-third Kentucky Infantry, and the Second Indiana Cavalry. They all joined us on the march next day, when we made an early start, and after proceeding six miles struck on the Lebanon Pike. About noon, passed through the small village of Liberty—a strong Union place. Going two miles further, we turned off on the road leading to Murfreesboro, and went into camp on the banks of Clear Creek. Remained here until 4 o'clock of the next afternoon, when we once more formed in line for the march.

On getting on the old road, we were faced towards McMinnville. The Thirty-first Indiana and Twelfth Kentucky, and Second Indiana Cavalry, remained in camp. Nine o'clock that morning, we arrived at our old camping ground at Smithville, and remained there for the night. Resumed marching early in the morning, and at 6 p. m. reached McMinnville. The day after our arrival at this place, the battery wagon, tents and baggage, came on from Murfreesboro. Remained here until Sunday afternoon, August 24th, when we again moved forward. The sick were sent to Nashville, and a large quantity of provisions and other property was buried, as there was not sufficient means of transportation.

At 3 o'clock the entire force were in motion. None but the officers in command knew our destination. We crossed the river, and found ourselves on the road to Altamont, Winchester, and other towns. Marched six miles, and, at 9 o'clock, halted for the night. It being late, and over a mile to where we could obtain water, and as all were tired and sleepy, we went to bed supperless—our beds being mother earth. Started early in the morning for Altamont, without breakfast. Proceeding two miles we came to water, and now supposed we would have a chance to cook our rations. But no; as soon as the horses were watered, "forward" was the word, and we must obey. This command caused much grumbling.

Two more weary miles were passed, when we again halted for a couple of hours; but no water was to be had here, so we were obliged to content ourselves with some dry, hard bread for breakfast. We finally got started again, and after going a short distance another halt was made, caused by the road being blockaded by the wagons. We at once turned into the woods on our left, and encamped. Remained here until daylight, and were once more ordered forward. Arrived at McMinnville at 11 a. m., and proceeded to our old camping ground, having been absent two days, and accomplished nothing. This was on August 26th. With the exception of an alarm, caused by some of the cavalry firing their guns just outside the lines, a few days after our return from the above expedition, nothing of note occurred until September 3rd.

On the morning of September 3rd—being just one month from our arrival—we took our departure from McMinnville. After the usual delay, we were on the move, and headed for Murfreesboro. For the past month we had been deprived of all communication with home, and had scarcely seen a paper. As a matter of course, we knew but little of what was transpiring in regard to the war. We could not even tell for what purpose we were ordered on, or what our destination. We marched about twelve miles this day, and then camped in a large open field.

During the morning we passed the place where a skirmish had taken place between some of our troops and a party of rebels, a few days previous. The Union force had succeeded in routing the enemy, but several of their men were captured. We remained in this camp until the next morning, and again started. At noon passed through Woodbury, and at night camped at Readyville, having marched about fifteen miles. The following morning resumed our march, and reached Murfreesboro at noon. Considerable delay was caused here, and it was 4 p. m. ere we pitched our tents, which was done two miles from town, on the Nashville Pike, and near Stone River.

Here, for the first time, we received information that some extraordinary movement was on foot. Troops, in large bodies, were constantly coming in from all quarters, and it seemed as if Buel's entire army were about to concentrate at this point, for the purpose of some grand movement upon the enemy. The report was that we were about to return to Kentucky. About this time we received a late paper, and the tenor of its news led us to believe that such a movement looked reasonable.

The next morning early were on the move towards Nashville. All doubts as to our course were now removed. Owing to the large body of troops in advance, our progress was necessarily slow. But we made sixteen miles during the day, which was September 6th, and at night camped at a small station on the Nashville and Chattanooga railroad, and fourteen miles from the former place.

An early start the next morning brought us, at noon, to within five miles of the city. We here turned off from the main road, and proceeding two miles, camped near a small creek. But scarcely had our picket ropes been extended, and horses unharnessed, when we were again commanded to move. This time proceeded to within a mile of the city, and then pitched our tents. Were ordered to be in readiness to move at 3 o'clock in the morning.

It was now evident that Kentucky was our destination. At the appointed time next morning, we were on the move; and, shortly after daylight, crossed the Cumberland River by means of the railroad bridge, which had been planked over for the purpose. We passed through the pleasant little town of Edgefield, and found ourselves on the road leading to Bowling Green. When we had gone four miles we halted in a piece of woods, and remained there two hours, then proceeded on our way, and at night camped eight miles from Nashville, and near what is called Edgefield Junction.

We remained at the above camping ground two days. On the afternoon of the 2nd of September, we had an alarm; and, as the surrounding country was swarming with rebels, it stood us well in hand to be on the alert. It took but a moment's notice to be prepared for action, when scouts were sent out in all directions. They succeeded in bringing in several prisoners, some of whom belonged to the rebel army. But little information could be obtained from them. The remainder of the day and night passed without anything further of note transpiring.

Early on the morning of September 11th, we were once more on the move. About 10 a. m. passed through the small town of Goodsonville, or Edgefield Station. We here saw evidences of the rebel's work of destruction. The place was almost entirely deserted, and every store had been completely riddled and robbed of its contents. Many of them had been fired, and were partially consumed.

We made no halt at this place, but continued our march. A few miles further on passed through another small town, which contained two or three stores, all of which were closed, and, as at Goodsonville, the inhabitants had mostly fled. At noon we halted near a large public house, where there was a fine spring of water. Here we procured dinner, and remained for two hours.

It appears that there had been a skirmish a short time previous, some two miles ahead, between our advance and a large body of rebel cavalry. A part of the Ninth Michigan Infantry, one section of Hewitt's Battery, and a small detachment of cavalry, succeeded in repulsing the enemy, who had one killed and three wounded, who fell into our hands. On our side, there was but one wounded.

About 2 o'clock resumed our march, and shortly after passed the spot where the skirmish had taken place. It was at a crossing of the road. We marched until 8 o'clock in the evening, and then camped near a small creek, where there were two or three stores.

September 12th resumed our march. We had skirmishers thrown out on each side of the road to prevent a surprise. Nothing worthy of note occurred during the day. Marched sixteen miles, and camped at Mitchellville shortly before dark. Had a light fall of rain during the night. General Buel joined us this day.

At daylight, September 13th, continued the march. At 10 a.m. arrived at Franklin, Kentucky, which place is on the Nashville and Louisville Railroad. It was reported that a large body of the enemy were hovering around the town. A halt was ordered, and scouts sent out in all directions. Each section of our battery went to the outer edge of the town on picket guard. After remaining one hour, and nothing seen or heard of the enemy, resumed our march. At 8 o'clock in the evening, camped two and a half miles from Bowling Green. Distance made this day, twenty-five miles.

Early the morning succeeding proceeded on the march, but went into camp one mile from Bowling Green. While here we suffered for the want of wholesome water—the only spring of good water being two miles from camp. We were obliged to use water for cooking purposes from a pond that was stagnant. Were kept on half rations, as we had been since leaving McMinnville. In place of hard bread, flour was distributed.

Were ordered to move on September 15th, but, after getting ready, the order was countermanded.

September 16th, again ordered to move, and at 5 o'clock

were ready, but waited two or three hours for the word to proceed. Finally started and went one mile, when we bivouacked on side of the road for the night, it being impossible to proceed further, owing to the immense wagon train.

At daylight next morning again started, and passed through the town of Bowling Green, and shortly after forded Barren River, then halted long enough for breakfast. About an hour before dark we left the turnpike, and turned off to the right, through a piece of woods. It now commenced raining quite hard, and the night was very dark. Our progress was but slow, and it was 10 o'clock ere we halted for the night. The rain was still falling heavily, and the air was quite chilly. Large fires was soon built, around which we all gathered to enjoy the genial warmth. Water was not readily obtained, and we lay down supperless. Tired and hungry, wet and cold, we were soon asleep.

The next morning, September 18th, opened cold and cloudy, but soon cleared up. And now, for the first time since leaving McMinnville, we had three days' full rations served out. Having found a mudhole, from which we could obtain water, all were soon busy in cooking their food, and for a time the camp was quite lively—the men once more wore cheerful faces, and our former hard fare was forgotten. Hardly, however, had we prepared our meal, when the order was given to move, and the grub went down our throats on a double quick. There was considerable "jawing" about that time.

In a few minutes, we were once more on the road. We started at noon, and for the greater part of the way the road lay through a woody and sparsely populated country. At dark we came in sight of camp fires, burning brightly, evidently but a short distance ahead. But, for some reason, we were delayed for hours on the road, and it was midnight ere we arrived at the place. Here was presented one of the most beautiful sights ever witnessed. Spread out in a large open space, extending over many acres of ground, were the campfires of an army of fifty thousand men. The fires were built in rows a few feet apart, each mess having its own fire. The men could be seen flitting about from point to point, some cooking, some carrying wood and water, some sleeping, others smoking or eating.

Occasionally the strains of a flute were wafted sweetly to the ear, borne on the night breeze. Then came the full manly chorus of some patriotic song, from one of the messes. Away in the distance we heard the sweet and touching words of "*Rock me to sleep, mother,*" sung by some brave but warm-hearted soldier-boy, as he thought of his dear home far away. Would that kind mother ever again fold her darling boy to her warm heart? Mayhap, even the morning's sun might shine on his lifeless form. The vicissitudes of war are great.

At a distance, the camp resembled a large and populous city by gaslight, and it was truly a magnificent spectacle. Our battery was soon joined with them, and most of us being wearied by the days' labours, lay down for a little sleep, as our orders were to move at daylight. We were informed that the place near which we were encamped was called Prout's Knob, from a small mountain, which reared its rugged head just outside the line of the encampment.

Were routed out before day next morning, September 19th, to prepare breakfast. At daybreak, were ready to move. General Smith now took the command of our division in place of General Ammon.

Owing to the large number of troops, it was nearly 7 o'clock before we got started. After proceeding four miles we halted in the road, and were kept there until 4 o'clock in the afternoon. During the day signal flags were kept flying, the meaning of which only those in command knew. At 4 o'clock we moved forward, and pitched tents in a field near the road, most of the infantry and other troops going further on.

Remained in camp during the day of September 20th, engaged in cooking three days' rations. While here heard of the fight at Mumfordsville, and defeat of our troops. All kinds of stories were at once set afloat, and, like those at a ladies' tea-party, were not much entitled to consideration. It was generally supposed that we were on the eve of a great battle.

At daylight, September 21st, were again ordered to move, and were soon on the road. But before we had gone one mile came to a halt. We turned aside into a piece of woods, where we remained till 5 o'clock in the afternoon, when we once more proceeded forward, and it was long past midnight ere we encamped, which was done near a small creek. Distance travelled, ten miles.

One o'clock, September 22nd, took the road, and after going some four miles came to where the enemy had been camped the night previous. It was reported that they had left in two divisions, and that some of our advance cavalry had a skirmish with them, and caused the enemy to retreat. We went about one mile further and were then ordered to "about face," it having been ascertained that we were on the wrong road. Going back two miles we turned to the left, and in a short time pitched tents on the banks of Green River, opposite Mumfordsville, and near an old fort which had been erected the previous winter.

September 23rd, again early on the march. At sunrise crossed Green River, and passed through Mumfordsville. At noon, halted near the railroad. Remained one hour, and once more under way. At 9 o'clock in the evening reached Camp Nevins, and pitched our tents near a creek. Marched this day twenty miles.

Early on the following morning moved forward. Passed through Elizabethtown without stopping. Went thirteen miles beyond, and camped for the night. We were now on a good macadamized road. As heretofore, water was scarce.

September 25th, resumed our march, and at noon arrived at West Point, situated on the Ohio, at the mouth of Salt River, and distant from Louisville twenty-two miles.

For the first time in a year we once more beheld a free State. After remaining a few hours, once more made a move. Crossed Salt River, and were now on the direct road to Louisville. Two miles from West Point we encamped.

Started before daylight, September 26th, and at noon reached Louisville.

CHAPTER 8

At Louisville—And Off Again

As before stated, at noon of September 26th, we arrived at Louisville, having marched over two hundred and fifty miles, occupying just twenty-three and a half days. We were nearly all worn out on this long, dreary, and tedious march, and presented a most woeful appearance, being dirty, ragged, and well nigh famished. Take it all in all, we had undergone more hardships and real suffering than on any previous occasion, and it was probably one of the most disastrous movements that had taken place since the war had an existence. The boys say it was a "masterly piece of military strategy," and think that a few more such movements will speedily terminate the war.

Our camp was located on a piece of low ground, and in a potato patch near the canal, through which the boats are obliged to pass when the river is at a low stage, as there is then an insufficiency of water on the falls.

We now had full rations served out, and as far as the matter of eating, were well off. On Sunday the 27th September, we received an addition of forty-seven new members, they having been recruited at Cleveland by Colonel Barnett and others. Two of our men, who had been home on sick leave, rejoined us at the same time.

On the afternoon of Tuesday, September 30th, we moved camp a short distance, and the same afternoon were paid for four months' services, and also received a lot of new clothing, which rendered the men extremely happy, and many a wistful eye was cast towards the city. But the same night we received that same "eternal" order to be ready to march the following morning. So the men were disappointed in the expectation of getting "shut" of their money.

At an early hour, October 1st, all were ready for a start; and shortly after daylight the battery was in motion. But, on crossing the canal, we came to a halt, and after being delayed an hour, again moved forward. In a short time another halt was ordered, and

We all halt, halt, halted.

In this manner nearly the entire day was consumed, and it was quite late in the afternoon ere we were fairly outside the city.

We now found ourselves on the Bardstown Pike, being the same road by which we had entered the city seven months previous. Marched six miles, and at 9 o'clock camped for the night.

October 2nd resumed our march at the usual early hour; but owing to the large force accompanying, our progress was slow. About 4 o'clock in the afternoon, and about eight miles distant from our starting point in the morning, heavy firing was heard some distance ahead, but in a short time it suddenly ceased. After proceeding two miles further we halted, and went into camp for the night. We soon learned, from scouts sent out, that the firing was occasioned by a skirmish between our advance and the rear guard of the enemy, who were slowly retreating before us. There being so many rumours concerning the skirmish, it was impossible to obtain a correct result. However, there was no great damage done on either side. The enemy, as usual, wanted to be "let alone." Considerable rain fell during the night.

Captain Standart and Lieutenant Bennett, who had remained at Louisville on business, joined us the next day, October 3rd. The morning was cloudy, with some rain. At 9 o'clock got started. The clouds swept away shortly after, giving place to the genial sun, and the remainder of the day was quite pleasant. At 10 a. m. passed through the small town of Mount Washington. Here was where the skirmish of the day previous had taken place. At 3 o'clock crossed a small stream, called Floyd's Fork. The bridge had been destroyed by the rebels. We had no difficulty in fording the stream, owing to the low stage of water. This was six miles from Mount Washington, and fourteen miles from Bardstown.

Just beyond here our advance cavalry were fired upon by the rebels, with artillery from a masked battery. A halt was at once ordered, and instant preparation made for action. Two of our guns, under command of Lieutenant Bennett, were moved forward some two miles, and were then fired upon. The pieces were immediately posted on a commanding place nearby, and opened on the enemy. A few shots were exchanged, when the firing soon ceased. Scouting parties were now sent out to reconnoitre, but returned without making any discovery of importance. Nothing more, worthy of notice, occurred during the night.

Having ascertained that the rebels had retired during the night, at 10 o'clock next morning, October 4th, we again moved forward. It was now evident that the enemy were gradually falling back, but had left a rear guard for the purpose of retarding our march, and to cause us as much trouble as possible, without bringing on a general engagement. About three miles from our last night's camping ground we again crossed Floyd's Fork, and near where the Lexington Pike intersects the Bardstown and Louisville road. We here found that the bridge had not been destroyed.

About one-half mile beyond we came to where the enemy had thrown up a sort of barricade against a fence, and from which they had, no doubt, intended to give us a surprise, but had thought better of the matter.

Another mile, and we came to a public building, called the Barclay House, and located on a high elevation. Here, the night previous, the rebels had posted their artillery. Our forces were again placed in position, and scouts sent out to ascertain the enemy's whereabouts. In two hours they returned without having made any discovery, and once more we resumed our march. At night camped within eight miles of Bardstown. From people living along the route we travelled, all manner of reports concerning the rebels were received. By some it was represented that they were at Bardstown, from sixty thousand to eighty thousand strong, and were going to make a stand to offer us battle. But little credence was given to any of these reports; but we were all inclined to believe that a battle was soon to be fought.

The morning of Sunday October 5th, was ushered in clear and pleasant. Had breakfast at daylight, and at 7 o'clock our column was in motion. We moved slowly, and with much caution, halting frequently. Once we laid by for nearly three hours. Shortly before dark we entered Bardstown, and found that the rebels had, as usual, "skedaddled." We now found that the detention during the day was caused by the arrival of another division of troops, who had come by a different road, and we had to wait for them to pass on ahead. We were informed by the citizens that the enemy had left but a few hours previous, and that the division above mentioned were in close pursuit. They had taken the direct road to Lebanon and Danville. We passed through town, took a road to the left—crossed a small creek, and pitched our tents, one mile beyond the place.

Early next morning, October 6th, again on the move. Our march this day was over a rough and hilly road, and through a thinly settled part of the country. At noon crossed a creek, the name of which we did not learn. Shortly after this we passed through the village of Glenville, and again got on a good road. Marched about eighteen miles this day, and, at 8 o'clock in the evening, camped one mile from Springfield.

October 7th. This morning continued our march, and at 8 o'clock passed through Springfield. A large party of rebels had been driven out of town the day previous, by the advanced division. We proceeded on towards Danville, following the pike for some distance, and then turned off to the left, on a common dirt road. Marched several miles, and at dark came out on the Lebanon and Danville road, six miles from the former place. General Gilbert's division passed on ahead. We went on two miles further, and, at a small village, turned off to the right, and proceeding some distance further, came to a creek, and camped. Our object in leaving the main road was to find water. Marched eighteen miles this day.

CHAPTER 9

Battle of Perryville

At 7 o'clock on the morning of October 8th, we resumed our march, returning and taking the Lebanon and Danville Pike. A few minutes after reaching the main road, we heard heavy firing some distance in advance. A halt was made, and the order given to transfer all extra baggage from the pieces and *caissons* to the baggage wagons, and be prepared for action. The report was then prevalent that the enemy were some five miles ahead, and had made a stand, and were already engaging our advance force. A fierce battle was now anticipated, and our men were anxious to participate in it, after the long chase we had given the enemy.

The firing had now become more frequent and distinct, and our men were becoming more and more eager for the conflict. As usual, there were all sorts of rumours regarding the number and position of the enemy. After a halt of one hour we again moved forward, and soon came on the Perryville Pike. Proceeding one mile further, we turned off into a field on the left of the road, and took position on a high piece of ground, our division being posted at different points. We held our position until near dark, when we moved forward half a mile, and were then stationed on a hill to the right of the road.

The fighting in the meantime had been most desperate, and was chiefly confined to General McCook's division, which maintained its ground in fine order, the men showing great bravery. The battle lasted until dark, when the enemy retired, and, on the following morning, retreated to Harrodsburg. The Union loss was eight hundred and twenty killed, between two thousand and three thousand wounded, and over four hundred missing. Enemy's loss, one thousand and eighty-two killed, and four thousand two hundred and sixty-one wounded. Our battery took no part in this action, as we were, during the time, out of range. It was the intention, on our part, to renew the battle the next day—the enemy willing—but they wanted to be "let alone," and withdrew from the field.

On the day following the battle, our battery was kept constantly on the move, charging through woods and cornfields, but no enemy was there. At night we camped near Perryville.

CHAPTER 10

Much Marching, but Little Fighting

The morning of October 10th were again early on the move, and at 9 o'clock passed through the town of Perryville, and proceeded on towards Danville. The buildings, as we passed along, presented the appearance of hard usage from the effects of the battle of Wednesday. Nearly every house was more or less riddled by shot and shell. We saw one house that seemed as if it had been the especial target of the gunners, for it was pierced in many places. We continued on for about two miles, when our advance had some little skirmishing with the enemy's rear guard. Our guns were at once drawn up in position on a high hill, having a good command of the country surrounding.

We remained here some fifteen or twenty minutes, and then proceeded forward on a double quick. Two miles further, and we came to a halt—all our forces being drawn up in line of battle. More skirmishing took place. About 4 o'clock we bivouacked in an extensive hemp field, four miles from Danville. The boys remarked that we had come here for the express purpose of preparing hemp for the "skedaddlers." That night was cold and stormy. We crawled under the hemp-stacks, and made ourselves as comfortable as the circumstances would admit.

October 11th. Morning still cold and stormy. We changed the position of our guns, and the horses were kept ready harnessed, and every one at his post. Some firing was heard on our left during the forepart of the day, and, in the afternoon, on our right. We, however, kept our position, and at night again slept under the hemp-stacks. The weather still continued cold, but the storm had ceased.

Weather next morning was clear, but cold. At 9 o'clock some of the enemy came into camp, bearing a flag of truce, but for what purpose we soldiers did not learn. About 10 o'clock we were ordered to move forward. Our march was through woods and fields, we seldom being on a regular travelled road. At 4 p. m. we came out on the turnpike leading from Danville to Camp Dick Robinson, and proceeded towards the latter place. The smoke of the enemy's campfires could be plainly seen. When within four miles of the camp we were ordered to "about face," and march back. So face about it was, and we were again passing over the same ground that we had but just travelled.

We marched boldly down the road,—
Then marched back again.

After going about three miles, we came out on another pike, which also led to Danville. And now we came to a halt, for the night. Supper was soon over with, and all turned in for a night's repose. Before midnight we were routed out, with orders to harness our teams and march. Soon found ourselves faced towards Danville. The night was clear and the road good, so we went along at a lively pace, and in an hour's time reached the town, and halted in a field just on the outskirts. We were now allowed to remain quietly until morning.

October 13th. The weather being fine, and as we were to remain in camp this day, the men took the opportunity to wash their clothes, it being the first time that they were able to do so since leaving Louisville. During the day we were visited by Colonel Barnett. We had not before seen him since leaving Nashville, in March, a period of eight months. Major Race also accompanied the colonel. At 4 o'clock we were ordered to move.

On getting into the road we found we were faced towards camp Dick Robinson. Marched three miles, and camped directly opposite the camping ground of the night previous.

On the following morning, October 14th, again on the move,

and going towards Danville, which place we reached about 9 o'clock a. m. We here turned into a field and halted. The entire army seemed in motion. After remaining here some two or three hours we again started, and about noon passed through town, and took the road leading to Stanford. Just before dark we turned off the main road, and after going two or three miles through the woods and fields, camped on a high piece of ground, as we supposed, for the night, as it was quite dark.

It was reported that a large wagon train of the enemy had passed only two or three hours in advance of us. As soon as supper was over those who were not on guard stretched themselves on the ground to seek repose. Suddenly the clear notes of the bugle rang out on the night air. Never was the sound more unwelcome; but its call had to be obeyed. The moon shone brightly, but the air was piercing cold. The prospect of an all night's march was not much relished.

As soon as we got out on the road we struck off on a double quick, and went spinning along towards Crab Orchard. Considerable firing was now heard some distance in advance. At every halt that was made fires were kindled with the rails along the road, and for miles ahead the sky was lighted up by them. There is something very impressive and thrillingly grand about a large army in motion at dead of night. The measured tramp, tramp, of the infantry, the rattle and creaking of artillery, the occasional neigh of a horse, mingled with the peculiar sound which always accompanies a large body—the breathing of thousands of human beings—and all lit up by the campfires, presents a weird, spectral scene. The march of death!

Shortly before daylight, and when we were some three or four miles from Crab Orchard, we came to a halt in the middle of the road. Several large fires were built, around which we all gathered. At daylight we got a cup of coffee and some "hardtack," then away on the road again. An occasional report of a gun could be heard. About 9 o'clock, a. m., we entered the town of Crab Orchard, and were here informed that the rear guard of the enemy had passed through only an hour before. The firing which we had heard was caused by a slight skirmish between them and our advance. Several prisoners had been taken.

After a few moment's halt we pushed on through the town, and once more were on the road to Wild Cat, the place where we had fought our first battle, nearly one year previous. The weather was fine, and the roads were in far better condition than when we first travelled them.

Proceeding four miles beyond Crab Orchard, our brigade left the main body, and turned off on a road leading to the left. Just before dark, and after having gone some six or eight miles, we were obliged to turn back, to find a suitable camping ground, as there were several high hills which we could not ascend at night. The road being very narrow, with a thick growth of trees and underbrush on either side, it was fully two hours ere we got fairly turned about. We then went one half a mile, and camped in a cornfield, near a small creek.

October 16th, resumed our march. Nothing worthy of note occurred during the day. About 3 p. m. passed through Mount Vernon. Did not make any halt. At night camped three miles from the crossing of Rock Castle River.

The next morning, early, moved forward, a part of the battery in advance. Captain Standart acted as a guide, from his previous knowledge of the country. He, with the advance, consisting of some cavalry and the Thirty-sixth Indiana Infantry, proceeded on some distance beyond Wild Cat, and on the road to London. When three miles beyond the old battle ground, they suddenly encountered quite a force of the enemy, when a brisk skirmish took place. In a short time our forces succeeded in driving the rebels, killing and wounding several of their number, and taking a few prisoners. Our loss was six or eight killed and wounded. Captain Standart had a very narrow escape, as one of the Thirty sixth Indiana was killed at his side.

Our entire battery, with the rest of the brigade, arrived at the summit of Wild Cat Mountain about 2 p. m. We then camped on the same place we had occupied on the first battle, and our guns were placed in almost the same position that they were in when we hurled death and destruction into the enemy's ranks nearly one year ago. Appearances indicated that we were to have another battle. It would indeed be a singular coincidence should we again fight on the old ground.

Our battery, being the only company of our present division that had participated in the former battle, was the centre of attraction, and many a tough "yarn" was told by our men of their exceeding valour at that time.

Lieutenant Bennett here left us to take command of a battery in Virginia.

During the day of October 18th, there was considerable movement among the troops, and, for a time, it seemed as if we were about to have an engagement. But still it was thought that the rebels would make for Cumberland Gap as speedily as possible. Some of our troops went out on the Winding Glade Road. Two of our guns were sent with them. Another body went towards London. Troops were constantly arriving. In the afternoon considerable firing was heard in the direction taken by our two guns. It was soon ascertained that a lively fight had taken place between our men and some rebel cavalry and infantry. Our troops soon drove them, taking about one hundred prisoners, and between two hundred and three hundred head of cattle. This occurred about four miles from Wild Cat. The enemy were driven some miles, and several of them were killed and wounded. Four men were wounded on our side.

About 10 o'clock, October 19th, were ordered to follow after the advance. A march of six or eight miles brought us to their encampment. It was located at what is called Scovill's Corners, or Cross-Roads, being where the Richmond road intersects the Lexington pike. We remained here during the night.

At 2 o'clock on the morning of the 20th, our battery was ordered out, to go on a reconnoisance, as was also the greater part of the brigade. All baggage-wagons, tents, and camp equipments, were left behind. The men took but one day's rations.

Shortly before daylight the brigade separated in two divisions, and proceeded out on different roads; but, after being absent all day without meeting with any of the enemy, with the exception of a few stragglers, whom they captured, they returned to camp. The rebels being alarmed at the near approach of our forces had hastily beat a retreat, burning several of their transportation wagons, to prevent their falling into Union hands.

October 21st. Just one year ago this day was fought the battle of Wild Cat; and we were only six miles from the place. All was quiet in camp.

Another reconnoisance was made, commencing October 22nd. Our battery went towards Manchester. The expedition was gone three days. Their object was to destroy the salt works near Manchester, on which the Rebels depended for a supply of that necessary article of consumption.

Having accomplished their purpose, and nothing further remaining to be done, the expedition returned to camp on the morning of October 25th. On the day previous, several citizens of London came into camp, and reported a large body of secesh cavalry in the town. It was thought that, owing to the absence of the greater part of our force, the rebels might take advantage of it, and make an attack on our camp during the night. Accordingly the men belonging to our battery were all armed with muskets, and given several rounds of ammunition. We were notified to hold ourselves in readiness to repel an attack.

For the first time our artillerymen were transformed into infantry. About one hundred refugees from East Tennessee came into camp, and were also armed. The night, however, passed without any alarm. Our troops arriving the next morning, we all again got in motion, and proceeded back through Wild Cat. Arrived at the Rock Castle River crossing, and camped for the night.

There was a very heavy snow storm during the night, and in the morning the ground was covered to the depth of several inches; but, the weather being mild, it rapidly disappeared. Got an early start, and pushed on through the mud and slush. At noon arrived at Mount Vernon, and halted for an hour in a large field, and cooked our dinner. At 2 o'clock we again moved forward, and went towards Somerset. The weather was now growing colder, and the snow had made the roads very heavy, so that our progress was but slow. It was a cheerless and comfortless march. Little do those at home, who tread only on hard, dry pavements, know where a soldier's feet hath been. We toiled on through the mud for about six miles, and then camped for the night. The snow was still quite deep, but we succeeded in getting some hay, and, clearing the ground, spread our blankets on the hay, then built large fires, and lay down to rest. Thus we managed to pass the night in tolerable comfort. It must be borne in mind that, as yet, we were without tents, and had been so ever since leaving Nashville.

The next morning, October 27th, we were up betimes, and, after breakfast, were again on the road. The sun shone brightly, yet the air was quite chilly. We marched about twenty miles, and at night camped near a small creek, two miles from Somerset.

The day succeeding we all remained in camp, and passed the time in looking over old letters—as dear to us as household words—and now and then a sly look was given to some well-worn miniature of a nameless friend far away in some northern home. Thus passed the day, and the stars came out, and

Sat their sentinel watch in the sky,

and found us sunk on the ground overpowered with sleep.

The following morning we were again on the march. Passed through Somerset at 8 o'clock, and went out on the road to Fishing Creek. Found all the places of business closed, and the town looking quite gloomy. The greater part of the inhabitants had left previous to the rebel army entering. We were warmly welcomed by those who remained—especially the members of our battery, as most of us were well known. As we passed the hill on which we had been so long quartered the previous winter, all eyes were turned towards it, and many a familiar spot was pointed out. It seemed to us like an old home.

We crossed Fishing Creek about 11 o'clock, a. m., and here remained until the following morning.

October 30th. Resumed our march, and, at 9 o'clock, a. m., passed the battle ground of Mill Springs.

Old stories of the battle were told, as we passed the familiar places where the conflict had raged. Many a tree bore the marks of cannon ball and shell. The fences were riddled with bullet holes, as evidences of the terrible work of January 19th, 1862, and which will long be remembered as an eventful day in future history.

We saw many graves of those noble heroes who that day gave up their lives in their country's cause. Peace to their ashes.

Marched about twenty miles this day, and camped near the road.

The next day we continued our march, and at dark crossed Green River, and camped one half-mile from Columbia, having marched twenty-one miles.

November 1st. Remained in camp. A general muster was had, for the purpose of making out the pay-roll. Weather clear and pleasant.

The next day resumed our march at noon, and, passing through Columbia at dark, camped near a creek, eight miles from last night's camp.

November 3rd. Again on the move, and at noon halted near the town of Edmonson, and remained long enough to feed horses and get dinner. Passed through the town, and took the road towards Glasgow. Marched eight miles, and camped in a piece of woods. The men had here a fine opportunity to gather hickory-nuts, which covered the ground profusely.

The next morning made an early start, and at noon passed through Glasgow, and camped one mile beyond.

We here found George Eldridge, with our baggage, tents, etc., which we had left behind at Bowling Green. Some of the sick, who had also been left, rejoined us here.

We remained in camp at this place for three days; and while here received some blankets, and a few articles of clothing, of which we stood greatly in need. Orderly Sergeant Kelley here received a commission as second lieutenant, and Sergeant Thompson was promoted to orderly. quarter-master's sergeant, George Eldridge, was transferred on detached service, as clerk in the Division Quarter-Master's department. The weather, during the time we remained here, was wet and disagreeable.

Saturday, November 8th. Broke up camp, and resumed our march towards Nashville. Marched about twenty miles, and camped near the road. During the day we crossed Great Barren River.

Next morning proceeded towards Scottsville, where we arrived at noon. Pitched tents one mile beyond, and remained until next day.

Scottsville is sixty miles distant from Nashville, and is the last town we passed through previous to entering Tennessee.

November 10th. Commenced our march at half-past 8 o'clock, a. m. At noon halted for dinner, a short distance from the boundary line of Kentucky and Tennessee. At 2 o'clock we were again on the move, and in the state of Tennessee, having been out of that state nearly two months. Marched only thirteen miles this day, and halted for the night. Weather clear and cold.

Early the next morning on the move. At half-past 3 o'clock, p. m., passed through Gallatin, without stopping, and took the Lebanon road. At night camped on the banks of Cumberland river, about three miles beyond Gallatin. Had all kinds of rumours during the day. One of which was that there had been a fight at Nashville. No reliance could be placed on these reports.

The morning of November 12th opened with a cold, drizzling rain. About 11 o'clock, a. m., we were ordered to move; and, after waiting until near noon for the Tenth Brigade to pass, we finally forded the river—which was at this time quite low— and marching eight miles, encamped for the night in the woods, near the Nashville and Lebanon turnpike.

The next morning, at 10 o'clock, we started towards Nashville, and on reaching Silver Springs, camped in rear of the town.

This place is distant eighteen miles from Nashville.

We remained here for several days, during which time one of our men was tried by court martial for attempting an outrage on the person of a woman in Kentucky, while on the march from Somerset to Columbia. He was found guilty, and sentenced to serve six months in military prison, with ball and chain attached to his leg, and to forfeit two months' pay.

While here, General Crittenden came near falling into rebel hands. He, however, managed to escape, but several of his staff were captured.

After having remained in camp at Silver Springs for six days, on the morning of November 19th we broke up, and moved down the turnpike towards Nashville. Proceeded as far as Stone River, and again camped, being eight miles from the city. We remained here one week, with nothing worthy of note transpiring.

Broke up camp on the morning of November 26th, and moved towards Nashville.

During the march, one of our new members, who had joined us at Louisville, named Leonard Starr, died in the ambulance. He had been sick several days. His remains were sent home in charge of his brother, who is also a member of our battery.

We camped on the Murfreesboro pike, three miles from Nashville.

Our tents were pitched in a large open field. The ground was low and springy, and whenever it rained, the place was almost untenable.

The day after our arrival was Thanksgiving day, but it passed off the same as all other days with us. We had our usual dinner of sow-belly *a la mode*, and hard-tack *a la mouldy*.

Nothing out of the usual course occurred, until December 8th. On that day, our brigade made a foraging excursion on the Nolensville pike. Went ten miles, and succeeded in obtaining one hundred and sixty-nine loads of corn, which was brought away in sight of the enemy's pickets, without a gun being fired.

Captain Standart was acting as chief of artillery on General

Palmer's Staff; General Palmer having succeeded General Smith as division commander.

I will here mention that we were now in what was called the Fourth Division of General Crittenden's Corps. Our brigade is known as the Twenty-second, General Cruft commanding. Lieutenant Baldwin, at this time, was temporarily commanding the Battery.

On the 10th, we moved our camp about one-fourth of a mile to a drier piece of ground. Captain Standart also moved his quarters back to the battery, but still retained his position as chief of artillery.

We remained in camp near Nashville just one month, during which time we had several alarms, but none of them of any consequence. Also made several reconnoisances on different roads.

We here received a supply of new clothing, harness, and other equipments; and, on the morning of December 24th, were ordered to have five days' rations in haversacks, ready to march— but for some cause did not move.

Christmas went by in quiet, but it was only a lull in the war-storm which was soon to break upon us with a fury hard to withstand.

On the morning of the 26th we were ordered to move. All camp equipage and baggage, as well as those who were not fit for active duty, were to be moved into Nashville.

The storm was about to burst.

CHAPTER 11

Skirmishing Previous to the Battle of Stone River

At an early hour on the morning of Friday, December 26th, the shrill call of the bugle ringing out on the frosty air, announced that we were about to move.

Soon great activity prevailed in camp, and all were in high spirits at the prospect of an advance; and it was evident to each and every one of us, that unless the rebels should retreat from Murfreesboro, a battle must soon occur.

Nothing so arouses a soldier's spirit as the prospect of a battle—though, in the same anxiously looked for battle, his life may be sacrificed. For human life, at best, but hangs on a thread which even a little blow may snap asunder. But if man dies thus, his life is nobly given on the altar of his country, and that is worth the life of any man.

Who dies in vain

Upon his country's war-fields, and within
The shadow of her altars?

War follows rebellion, and death follows war. Some must die—both the just and the unjust; but in the end, right will *ever* conquer. And now to our movements.

The morning was cloudy, and in a short time it began to rain. Nevertheless, all were soon ready to move. After waiting for more than an hour, the command was finally given to "forward march."

The army of General Rosencrans had now been divided into three separate divisions, or army corps, and designated as the right, left and centre wings. The right, commanded by General McCook; the centre, by General Thomas; and the left, by General Crittenden. To the last named was our battery attached, General Palmer being still in command of the division, and General Cruft of the brigade. Our corps moved forward on the Murfreesboro road, the other corps taking different routes. At the time we got fairly started the rain had increased, and the storm was raging furiously; and though all were thoroughly drenched, yet it dampened not the ardour of the brave men, as they were elated at the prospect of soon meeting their deadly enemy in battle array.

Owing to the great number of troops, and having a large wagon train, our progress was quite slow; and further, it was known that our movements would be more or less harassed by the enemy. Great caution was therefore necessary.

When within two miles of Lavergne—which is a small station on the Nashville and Chattanooga Railroad—our advance guard encountered the rebel pickets. After a short skirmish, the enemy were driven into their camp at Lavergne, where they had one brigade stationed.

Our brigade having the advance, we soon came in sight of the enemy, who were drawn up in line ready for battle. Our battery, and one section of Konkle's Battery, under command of Lieutenant Nathan Newell, were ordered into position, and opened on the rebels. They immediately returned our fire, when a lively artillery fight commenced, which lasted until dark. One of our men had his hand badly shattered, by the premature explosion of one of the guns. He has since had his hand amputated. One of the men belonging to Newell's section was instantly killed by the rebel fire. This was the only loss sustained on our side. The rebels suffered the loss of a number killed and wounded, and a few taken prisoners.

Early next morning, we were in readiness to renew the attack; but the enemy were not inclined to oppose us, as they commenced a retrograde movement towards Murfreesboro. Our troops at once pressed on them closely, and constant skirmishing ensued throughout the entire day. At dark, we had succeeded in driving them six miles, to what is called Stewart's Creek. We here rested for the night—the rebels on the east and we on the west side of the creek.

The following day both armies remained in the same position, and no movement was made on either side. *We* were awaiting the arrival of General Thomas' troops.

The next morning we moved forward in order of battle. Skirmishers were thrown out on each side of the road, through the woods and fields, and during the day some little fighting took place. We moved to within four miles of Murfreesboro, and camped for the night in a piece of cedar woods.

The following day was passed in preparing for the great battle, which was now imminent. Our troops were posted at different points, Batteries placed in position, picket lines established, scouts and skirmishers thrown out, ammunition chests overhauled, and all other necessary preparations made for the coming conflict.

That night our guards were doubled. The infantry slept on their arms, and artillerymen at their several posts. No fires were allowed, and the utmost vigilance enjoined on all.

Tomorrow would be an eventful day.

CHAPTER 12

The Battle of Stone River

FIRST DAY

Just at daylight, and while some were getting breakfast, others watering their horses, the rebels made a sudden and vigorous attack on the division of General Johnson in General McCook's Corps, and which was stationed on the extreme right.

Owing to the suddenness of the attack, and the overpowering force which the enemy had brought to bear at this particular point, the troops of General Johnson were thrown into confusion, and ere they could recover from their surprise, the enemy had broken through their lines, and forced them to fall back, at the same time firing volley after volley, killing and wounding a large number of Union troops. They had also succeeded in capturing several pieces of artillery, and, in one instance, the entire battery of Captain Edgarton, taking the captain and most of his men prisoners.

General Johnson rallied the remainder of his troops as speedily as possible, and others coming to his support—but not until having lost considerable ground—by 9 o'clock, a. m., the engagement had become general along the entire line. At 10 o'clock the battle raged with great fury, and slaughter. Our battery was stationed on the left of General Negley's division—it being the last, or left division of the right wing. The enemy, at noon, had succeeded in turning this wing, and had partially got in on our rear, subjecting us to a severe cross-fire. General Cruft, however, managed to extricate the brigade from this unpleasant predicament, and our battery was drawn off in fine order, but not until we had expended all our ammunition. Our men, as well as those of the entire brigade, stood their ground bravely, and dealt dire destruction to the enemy. Several of our men were killed and wounded about this time.

The battle still raged with great fierceness. The rebels had gained a great advantage, and had driven General McCook's wing two or three miles.

At this critical juncture, when it seemed as if we must suffer complete annihilation—when the rebel star was in the ascendant—Generals Rosencrans and Thomas came dashing along the line, cheering and rallying their men, when they turned and fought like very tigers. And now the scene was truly thrilling.

Then more fierce

The conflict grew; the din of arms—the yell
Of savage rage—the shriek of agony—
The groan of death, commingled in one sound
Of undistinguished horrors.

Inch by inch was the lost ground recovered, as hand to hand friend and foe grappled for the mastery. General Rosencrans, by his dauntless bearing, cheered on our brave men to such deeds of valour as the pen of history has seldom recorded. Fiercely did the Union troops throw themselves in solid battalions against the fierce assailing foe. The roar of artillery, the rattle of musketry, the groans of the wounded and dying, rang horribly upon the ear.

Darkness finally closed over the scene, and, for the time, put an end to the conflict. Weary and exhausted the men threw themselves on the blood-dyed ground, to pass the hours of night, their ears filled with the groans of their dying companions.

The number of killed and wounded, on both sides, this day, was quite large.

Thus ended the old year of eighteen hundred and sixty-two.

Second Day

The New Year dawned not on faces radiant with joy and gladness; for, alas! many of our brave comrades lay stark and cold on that ensanguined field. No "Happy New Year" came from their voiceless lips—no kindly word of greeting; but, with eyes upturned to Heaven, they lay mute in death. Never again would that gray-haired father welcome his son on the threshold of home. Never again would that meek-eyed mother fold her darling soldier-boy to her heart. Never again would brother, nor sister, gaze upon his manly form—for that brave boy slept his last sleep on the battlefield of his country. Who shall say that the angels did not welcome him that morning to a Happy New Year, where the sound of battle is never heard?

No, there were no merry greetings, nor lively pealing of bells, for those war-worn men; but instead was heard the roar of artillery, and the rattle of musketry, and the groans and shrieks of the wounded and dying soldier, mingled with that thrilling and strange cry of the horse on receiving his death wound.

The fighting this day was confined principally to artillery, but at longer range than the day previous, and consequently the slaughter was much lighter.

The battle lasted through the day, with no material advantage to either side; and at night both armies retained nearly their positions of the morning.

Another night was passed on the battlefield.

Third Day

Early the following morning considerable skirmishing ensued, and continued through the forenoon, with shifting of positions.

Between 3 and 4 o'clock in the afternoon, the rebels, in strong force, opened an attack on a single brigade of ours, which was posted near Stone River, and in advance of our extreme left. Pressed by greatly superior numbers the brigade was compelled to fall back, which they did in good order, contesting every inch of ground, and making great havoc in the enemy's ranks. Our reserve force soon pushed forward, with cheers and yells, determined to do or die. With a shock that could not be withstood, our brave men rushed upon the foe. Their columns shook—they wavered, reeled, and fighting desperately, fell back, while the brave Union troops pushed them at every step. Vainly did the rebel general in command strive to rally and turn back his horror-stricken legions. But furiously, more furiously, did our noble men assail the rebellious foe, till the ground was piled heap on heap with the slain, and the thirsty earth drank up their life blood. And now, in utter confusion, the enemy gave way, and soon were flying before us, like chaff before the wind.

Night had now set in, and darkness was gradually stealing over us; but still we fought on, determined to achieve a glorious victory for our country, and our firesides.

Our forces were now massed, and with cheers that made the welkin ring, we charged down upon a battery of artillery, which had been pouring destruction into our ranks.

So great was this onset, that again did the enemy give way and retire from their guns, and fled in wild disorder back into the cedar thickets which dotted the battle-field.

In this charge we captured four guns of the enemy's celebrated Washington Battery, of Louisiana, and also recaptured several of our own guns, which were taken from us in the first day's fight.

The rebel loss, in killed, wounded, and prisoners, was nearly three to our one. Had but two hours more of daylight intervened, the rebel army would have been well nigh annihilated. It was fortunate for them that darkness put an end to the conflict, when

Our bugles sang truce—for the night-cloud had lower'd,
And the sentinel stars set their watch in the sky;
And thousands had sunk on the ground overpower'd,
The weary to sleep, and the wounded to die.

Thus passed another night on the battlefield.

During this day the enemy kept up a continual skirmishing along our front, but without seeming inclined to risk another general encounter. This afterwards appeared to have been only a blind to cover their retreat, for during the same night they evacuated the field.

On Sunday morning, January 4th, General McCook entered Murfreesboro, and took formal possession of the town.

Thus ended the great Battle of Stone River, which, for desperate and hard fighting, has not been excelled by any battle fought during the rebellion.

SUMMARY

It would be occupying too much time and space to give full particulars of all that transpired during this memorable conflict. And where all fought so bravely and so well, it will not be necessary to discriminate. Taken as a whole, it was one of the hardest contested, and most decisive battles, which has yet been fought. The loss, in killed and wounded, on both sides, was very heavy. The enemy's loss, in killed and wounded, will not vary far from twelve thousand to fourteen thousand. About five thousand of the enemy fell into our hands as prisoners of war. We captured but few arms or equipments. Our loss, in killed and wounded, was about eight thousand, and from three thousand to four thousand captured and missing. The rebels probably gained a slight advantage in the amount of artillery captured. Several generals, and other officers high in rank were killed and wounded, on both sides. The rebels retreated towards Tullahoma.

This victory once more placed us in possession of a good part of Middle Tennessee, and thereby materially afforded us help in obtaining supplies.

The enemy were confident of success, but were woefully disappointed, and it has been a severe blow to them, and one from which they will hardly recover. General Rosencrans rather outwitted the redoubtable rebel Bragg, and came off with increased laurels. Rosencrans has shown himself to be the right man in the right place. He knows no such word as *fail*.

Our battery, in this engagement, was in command of Lieutenant Norman Baldwin. Captain Standart was still acting as Chief of Artillery, on General Palmer's Staff. Lieutenant Sypher was sick, at Nashville. Both Lieutenants Baldwin and Sturges acted with great coolness and bravery. Lieutenant Baldwin had one horse killed under him.

The battery was several times in a dangerous position, and once was nearly surrounded by the enemy, and subjected to a severe cross fire. The men heroically stood at their posts, and fought like veterans, while the air was hissing with shot and shell. None wavered from their duty, and all are deserving of the highest praise. But, alas! some laid down their lives in that fearful battle-storm. This was the first time that any of our company were killed in battle.

The following is a list of the members of the battery who were killed, wounded, and taken prisoners:

Killed—Orderly Sergeant Thomas J. Thompson; Sergeant George Wolf; Privates Chauncey Lyon, Samuel Ruple, John Elliott.

Wounded Seriously—Privates Benjamin F. Sarles, S. W. Shankland, William Broe, Alfred French John Blanchard.

Wounded and Missing—A. J. McLaughlin, George Overy.

Slightly Wounded—L. L. Sawtell, N. Schoh, J. Arndt, J. Grant, —. Hayes.

Of those mentioned as killed, Chauncey Lyon was killed instantly; Sergeant Wolf had his head entirely blown off, and, as is supposed, by one of our own guns, as he was seen to step in front of the battery just as the command to fire was given. Immediately thereafter his lifeless body was found near one of the guns. The others died a few days after, from the effects of their wounds.

Those seriously wounded were removed to the hospitals at Nashville. Alfred French had his arm amputated. The others will all probably recover without loss of limbs. Those who were slightly wounded continued on duty. We had twenty-one horses killed. A shot struck the forge, knocking out a spoke and splintering the box. The battery wagon was made a complete wreck.

CHAPTER 13

We Leave the Battlefield

We remained camped on the battle-ground until the 7th of January, when we moved about three miles beyond Murfreesboro, on the McMinnville road, and camped in a piece of woods near the road. The same night the wagons came out from Nashville, bringing our tents and baggage. We remained here through the next day. On Friday, January 9th, we struck tents, and went one mile nearer town.

We camped about a quarter of a mile off the road, and near a house. The ground was not very well adapted for such a purpose, being quite low.

During our stay here we experienced much heavy weather; it rained or snowed a great portion of the time. But we now received a supply of new clothing, and other necessary articles.

After remaining here for ten days, on the morning of Sunday, January 18th, we once more made a move.

The morning was quite cold, and considerable snow lay on the ground—a heavy snow storm having prevailed during the night.

A march of six miles brought us to Cripple Creek. We pitched our tents on a hill overlooking the surrounding country, and near the creek. The place was very rocky, and covered with young cedars. The trees, rocks and stumps, were so thick that it was almost impossible for a wagon to get through. But the men went to work, and soon had the ground sufficiently cleared to pitch the tents. This camp was on the McMinnville road, and eight miles from Murfreesboro. We had passed the place several times previously.

The day succeeding our arrival all hands went to work clearing up the ground, felling trees, and building breastworks and fortifications. This occupied several days. The weather was cold, with frequent rains, which rendered our condition rather unpleasant.

Nothing out of the usual way occurred until January 24th, when the entire brigade made a reconnoissance towards Woodbury. On reaching Readyville were joined by General Hazen's brigade, and then proceeded as far as Woodbury, where a skirmish ensued with a small rebel force. Our troops repulsed and drove them from the town. Our brigade returned to camp the same night.

Sunday, January 22nd. This being the anniversary of Washington's birthday, at sundown we fired a salute.

The next day Captain Standart started for home, having obtained a short furlough.

March 2nd. A skirmish reported beyond Readyville.

March 3rd. The entire division of General Reynolds passed our camp, going towards Woodbury.

March 5th. An election took place for five persons whose names should be placed on the Roll of Honour, according to published order of General Rosencrans. The following men were elected, *viz*: John Boon, Joseph Axford, Thomas C. Potter, John Snyder, and C. B. Valentine.

March 6th. Were paid this day for four months' services, being up to January 1st. The first payment we had received in six months. This put the men in good spirits again; but they had one difficulty, and that was, they had no means of getting rid of their money, as the market in this vicinity was not over-well stocked with what a soldier wants.

The next day a portion of General Reynold's force—which went towards Woodbury a few days previous—returned to

Murfreesboro. Cannonading was heard this day—supposed to be in the direction of Franklin.

The morning following, the order was passed to prepare to march. But, after getting ready, we stood all day waiting for the word to proceed. Just at dark were told to unharness horses, as we were not to move for the present.

Tuesday, March 10th. All quiet on Cripple Creek. Tents were again pitched. Considerable rain fell during the day.

Thursday, March 12th. Lieutenant Baldwin went to Nashville this day, to procure horses.

Saturday, March 14th. Buchanan Reed, the artist and poet, of Cincinnati, addressed our brigade this day. Lieutenant Kelley left for home, having resigned, and his resignation being accepted. Captain Standart returned to his command.

Sunday, March 15th.—Eighth week in our present camp. Brigade review today.

Sunday, March 22nd. Ninth week in camp.—Weather delightful. Peach trees in bloom. Trees leaving out.

Wednesday, March 25th. Received news to-day that George D. Eldridge—a member of our company—was dead. He died in hospital, at Nashville.

Sunday, March 29th. Tenth week in camp. Last night, at 10 o'clock, we had an alarm. It was caused by our pickets, who fired on a small party of rebel cavalry—the cavalrymen having made a dash on them, so the pickets reported. No one hurt.

Wednesday, April 1st. At 12 o'clock last night were routed out, with orders to prepare three days' rations, in haversacks, for a reconnoissance. Two hours later preparations were completed, when a start was made. All of our guns were taken, with two train wagons. The forge and battery wagons, and all camp equipage, were left in camp. The brigade divided and took different roads. The object of this movement was to surprise and capture a force of rebel cavalry, who were camped between Woodbury and McMinnville. A part of the third brigade came out to our camp, on guard duty, during the absence of our brigade. The expedition returned at night, having dispersed the enemy, killing and wounding a number. They also captured their entire camp equipage, several wagons, a lot of horses and mules, and about twenty prisoners.

The next morning the third brigade of our division passed camp. Part of the Fifteenth Pennsylvania Cavalry were with them. They had no camp equipage, and carried five days' rations. Were on a reconnoissance, and going towards Woodbury and McMinnville.

Saturday, April 4th. Part of our brigade went to Readyville, as guard to General Hazen's camp.

Sunday, April 5th. Eleventh week in camp.

Tuesday, April 7th, were paid today up to 1st of March.

Saturday, April 11th. At roll-call we had orders to draw three days' rations, and be in readiness to move at daylight next morning.

Sunday, April 12th. All were ready to move, but no further order was given in regard to doing so. In the afternoon the First and Second Kentucky Infantry were each presented with a beautiful flag. The weather continued fine. This was our twelfth week in present camp.

Monday, April 20th. General Reynold's division passed our camp on another reconnoissance towards Woodbury and Mc-Minnville.

Tuesday, April 21st. The men were this day—as well as several days previous—engaged in clearing up camp—hauling gravel and evergreens. The ground had been levelled off, and covered with gravel, and arbours and summer-houses built of evergreens, stables made for the horses, and our camp otherwise beautified. It now presented a cheerful appearance. From indications it appeared that we were to remain here for some time to come. We were favoured with fine weather—but little rain having fallen during the last month. Everything in nature looked beautiful.

Saturday, April 25th. A teamster belonging to the brigade, while intoxicated, fell off his mule just in front of our camp. The wagon passed over him, injuring him so severely that he died the same night. Could not learn his name, nor to what regiment he belonged.

Sunday, April 26th. Fourteen weeks this day since our arrival here. Lieutenant Baldwin started for home, on a short furlough. Lieutenant Sypher was sent to Cleveland, on recruiting service, on the 22nd inst. The teamster who was killed the day previous was buried this day.

Tuesday, April 28th. Had orders to hold ourselves ready to move at any moment. Considerable rebel cavalry were daily seen hovering around our lines. Nothing very serious apprehended.

Thursday, April 30th. Regular two month's muster for pay. Our tents were also turned over to the quarter-master. We were to have what are termed "shelter" tents, in place of our old ones. The men call them "dog" tents, and they are rightly named. Although this was the day set apart, by President Lincoln, as a day of fasting and prayer, everything went on as usual in camp. The men said that they had done enough fasting.

Friday, May 1st. All the sick were this day sent to the hospital.

Sunday, May 3rd. Fifteen weeks this day at Cripple Creek. We were joined by two companies of the First Tennessee Cavalry. They went into camp on the flats across the creek. Regular brigade review.

Monday, May 4th. The One Hundred and Twentieth Illinois Infantry passed our camp, going towards Murfreesboro. The regiment had been for some time in the Second brigade of General Palmer's division, but had been reduced by sickness and desertion, so that it did not then contain over one hundred and fifty effective men. The weather continued quite warm.

Tuesday, May 5th. The Twenty-Third Kentucky Infantry passed our camp, on their way to take the place of the One Hundred and Tenth Illinois. Weather cloudy, with some rain.

Friday, May 8th. Lieutenant Baldwin returned from home, bringing numerous packages for the men, sent by their friends.

On Sunday, May 11th, J. P. Beers died, at noon. His disease was Typhoid fever. He hailed from Collamer, a few miles East of Cleveland, Ohio. At 3 o'clock a grand review of the entire brigade took place, after which the troops were formed in a hollow square, when Captain Standart was called out and presented, by General Cruft, on behalf of the officers of the brigade, with a beautiful flag for our battery. But great was the captain's surprise, when the General presented him with a splendid sword, as a mark of the respect and high estimation in which the officers of the brigade held him. General Cruft then made a neat little speech, which was happily responded to by Captain Standart.

Colonel Barnett being present, also offered a few remarks, in which he alluded, in a happy manner, to the good discipline and soldierly bearing of the men, and congratulated us for the fair name and reputation which we had gained.

Colonel Enyart, of the First Kentucky Infantry, was also presented with an elegantly wrought sword, by the officers and soldiers of his command.

Immediately after the above ceremony, loud, long, and hearty cheers were given for General Cruft, Colonel Barnett, Captain Standart, Colonel Enyart, and the officers of the First Brigade. And now all quietly marched back to their respective quarters.

Sunday, May 10th, 1863, will long live in the remembrance of those who composed Standart's Battery.

The flag which we received was made of the most costly material. On its folds, in letters of silver, was inscribed:

Presented by the Officers of First Brigade, Second Division, Twenty-First Army Corps, to Standart's Ohio Battery.

Underneath this were the Words: Wild Cat, Mill Springs,

Chaplin Hills, Stone River. The captain's sword is heavily mounted with gold, and is a beautiful piece of workmanship. It cost two hundred dollars.

From the above it will be seen that the services which our Battery has rendered in the Union cause are duly appreciated by those who know our history best.

The morning succeeding the above eventful day, the body of J. P. Beers was sent home. The detachment to which he belonged escorted his remains outside the lines.

The day following, the Third brigade of our division arrived, and camped near us.

Friday, May 15. A little excitement in camp, caused by a horse-race for one hundred dollars a side. Our whilom mule-driver says that his steed can run the "har" clean off them dandi-fied looking "critters." But says he don't "keer" about betting, as cabbages ain't very plenty just now.

Sunday, May 17th. On this morning, as General Palmer and staff were out, with some of the First Tennessee cavalry, on a reconnoissance, when about five miles from camp they were suddenly confronted by a large body of Rebel cavalry, who at once opened fire on them. General Palmer gave the command for his cavalry to charge, and which order the brave Tennesseans were not slow in obeying. With drawn sabres they rushed on the rebels, which caused them to give way, when they broke and fled in confusion. The result was the capture of about twenty prisoners, the same number of horses, and a few muskets. Two captains were among the prisoners. One or two of the enemy were killed, and several wounded. Two or three slightly wound-ed on our side. The prisoners were soon after brought into camp. Brigade inspection in the afternoon. Seventeen weeks in camp at Cripple creek.

After the above incident nothing aside from the usual daily routine and an occasional reconnoissance, transpired until Tues-day, June 23rd. On this day we received word that Andy Ives, a member of our company, was dead. He had been sick for some time, and had been taken to Nashville by his father. This made twenty-two of our members who had died or been killed since we first entered the service. This afternoon the entire army in camp at Cripple Creek was called out to witness the execution of a private, in the First Kentucky Infantry, for desertion.

At half-past 2 o'clock, p. m., the division marched in regiments to the parade ground, and were drawn up in the usual manner on such occasions. At a quarter to 3 o'clock the prisoner made his appearance, following his coffin, and surrounded by a strong guard. On either side of him was a chaplain, or spiritual adviser. The drums beat a mournful march, and, after passing around the various regiments, with head uncovered, the doomed man was placed behind his coffin. He was then allowed to make a short address, but little of which could be heard. After he had concluded, a prayer, in his behalf, was offered by each of the chaplains. The prisoner then shook hands with them, and with some of the officers. His eyes were then bandaged—his bosom bared for the fatal shot. The soldiers detailed for this painful duty took their positions. With a suspense which was painful to witness, all awaited the final word for the execution.

Precisely at 3 o'clock the signal was given, and immediately the report of twelve guns echoed through the valley. . . . . . All was over.

On examination it was found that four balls had pierced his heart, and one had entered his temple. His death was easy and instantaneous.

Thus ended a sad and painful scene, the like of which we hope never again to behold. The man's name was Shockman, and he hailed from Cincinnati. He was about twenty-eight years of age, and unmarried.

On returning to our quarters, an order was received to issue twelve days' rations, and be ready to move at a moment's notice. As we had before received such orders, and nothing came of them, the men were now inclined to believe—as we had been so long at this camp—that we would here remain until disbanded. But at dark it became quite evident that a move would be made on the following morning. Some were pleased at this, but others were loth to leave a place which had become almost like a home to them. We had now been here a little over five months—by far the greatest length of time we had remained in any one camp. But all things must have a termination, and so did our stay here.

In the different dates above, have been given the items of interest which occurred during our stay at Cripple Creek. But little else, aside from the usual routine of camp life, had taken place.

CHAPTER 14

Departure from Cripple Creek

Early on the morning of June 24th all were astir, and busily engaged in preparing to march. The word was given to be ready at 7 o'clock. The weather was quite cloudy, and indicated rain. At 8 o'clock it commenced raining; and shortly after, we were on the move, having bid *adieu* to Cripple Creek, which had so long been our home. The rain was now falling heavily, and so continued through the whole day.

After crossing the creek, we took a South-east course. The roads in many places were quite rough, but the country, generally, was level. We passed through a fine farming section, and the crops mostly looked flourishing, but somewhat backward, owing to the late spring frosts, which had delayed planting.

A march of six or eight miles brought us out on the Murfreesboro and Bradyville Pike, and the roads were now in better condition. General Wood's Division were here waiting for us to pass. A little further on, we found the Second Brigade, General Hazen, waiting to join us. Shortly after, we passed through the small town of Bradyville. About one mile beyond this, at a creek, a skirmish took place between some of the First Tennessee Cavalry and a party of rebel cavalry. Two of the Tennesseans were wounded, and, as usual, the enemy "skeedaddled."

A halt was now made; and, after standing in the rain for an hour, we finally turned off the road, and camped for the night in a piece of woods. Thus ended our first day's march from Cripple Creek.

The next morning was again rainy. Made a move at 6 o'clock, and found the roads rough and hilly. Had one very steep and bad hill to ascend, and found it necessary to double our teams; but it was some time ere all the guns and caissons were well at the top. We marched about five miles, and then halted for the wagon train to come up. The weather had now partially cleared. At 5 o'clock, seeing no prospect of the trains arriving that night, we finally camped. Some firing heard in the distance, on our left.

Next morning, the train had not reached us, and we could not move without it, as we were without provisions or forage. Were obliged to send back for feed for our horses. More rain was falling, and the roads were getting very heavy. About noon, the wagons arrived; but no further move was made, and we quietly remained in camp. Heavy firing was heard nearly all day. A general battle was reported as going on at Beech Grove, about twelve or fourteen miles distant. General Thomas' corps was engaged. Rumours were rife in camp, and several prisoners were brought in. Our camp was located at Holly Springs, about seventeen miles from Murfreesboro.

Saturday, June 27th. All hands were up at daylight, and prepared breakfast. The weather again cloudy. Firing on our right, still heard; but just before noon, ceased. At 12 o'clock, report came that General Thomas had defeated the rebels and driven them, taking a large number of prisoners, and a lot of plunder.

At 1 o'clock, we once more got started, but the road was in a horrible condition; and after plodding slowly along for some six miles, we turned into a field near a creek and pitched our tents.

Sunday, June 28th. Morning cloudy. About 9 o'clock it commenced raining, but we were soon moving. Went two miles, and then prepared to camp; but the stumps and brush were so thick that it was some time ere we were enabled to pitch the tents. This was one mile from Manchester, and near a large creek, called the Barren Fork of Duck River.

In the morning we were again moving, but nothing worthy of note transpired for several days.

Saturday, July fourth, eighteen hundred and sixty-three. This is the eighty-seventh anniversary of our national independence, and here we are engaged in civil war. What would our old revolutionary heroes say, could they but look in upon us? Ah! little did they dream when they laid down the sword and gun, that this country would ever again have cause to maintain her honour by sword-blade and cannon's mouth; yet, this curse has been entailed upon us, by the vandal hand of the South. And now, to-day we stand up in a cause just as pure and holy as that for which our fathers fought in days gone by. We battle for our country as a whole; it *must not,* it *cannot* be divided. Yes,

> *We'll battle for our own true flag,*
> *We'll fight for every star;*
> *In town, on plain, or beetled crag,*
> *Our cause we'll thunder far.*

But, already a light—faint though it be—breaks over our war-tossed homes, and 'tis slowly but surely expanding. Ere another year be passed, we hope to see its effulgent rays light up all the dark corners of our land. That light, is the light of Liberty and Union.

But to our battery.

We were now camped in the woods near Elk River, and there was but little prospect of our very soon getting out, as it rained almost uninterruptedly for several days, making our condition far from enviable. Our wagons, which had been left at Manchester, arrived early in the morning, as also did the train from Murfreesboro with provisions, which was hailed with delight. But still we were to be kept on half rations, as we had been for some time back.

During the afternoon the writer of this received two boxes of "good things" from home, and the men all gathered around him with open mouths and straining eyes.

There being a little "mountain dew" in one of the boxes, on inspection, it made some of the men feel in better spirits, and rather more patriotic.

Thus passed the 4th of July, 1863.

Tuesday, July 7th. About five o'clock in the afternoon cannonading was heard in the direction of Tullahoma, and from the regularity of the firing it was supposed to be occasioned by some good news. In a short time after, firing was heard much nearer, and evidently in General Thomas's corps, which was encamped on the opposite side of Elk River. One half hour later, the joyful news was received of the capture of Vicksburg, and the entire Rebel army of that place. The news spread like wild-fire through the camp, and everyone was in high glee. Good news was also received from the army of the Potomac, which was now under the command of Major-General Meade.

Wednesday, July 8th. Early this morning received word to prepare for a move. Some of the batteries in our division fired a salute in honour of the victory achieved at Vicksburg. About half-past 7, we got started, and moved towards Manchester. The roads were in a horrible condition, and it was with difficulty that we were enabled to proceed. We passed through the town of Hillsboro, and here General Woods's division went into camp while we pushed forward, and at 4 o'clock in the afternoon reached Manchester, a small town on the Chattanooga and Nashville railroad, and went into camp.

Our tents were pitched on the same ground that we formerly occupied, and on the following day we commenced clearing up and regulating the place, as it was evident that we were to remain here for several days. Shades of evergreens were erected over the tents, and the ground being hard and dry our situation was quite pleasant.

On Monday, July 13th, Generals Rosencrans and Crittenden, together with several other distinguished officers, arrived on the cars. They appeared to be on a tour of inspection; but after a short stop proceeded to McMinnville.

The pay master arrived on the following Wednesday, and took up quarters with Captain Standart. The next day we were paid for four months' services, being up to July 1st.

The above comprises about all that occurred while in camp at Elk River, out of the usual course of camp life. The weather, while here, was quite hot, and frequent thunder storms ensued. Several prisoners were brought in at different times, and numerous foraging expeditions were sent out, and were generally successful, bringing in oats, rye, and hay. Farmers came in with wagon loads of potatoes, fruit and vegetables, which were readily bought by the soldiers. A number of men in our battery built ovens, in which they baked bread, pies, etc.; and, as a general thing, we lived on the best the country afforded.

A few days before we left camp an addition was made to our battery of twelve new members, who were enlisted on the Western Reserve, in Ohio. Orderly Sergeant Thompson, received his commission as Second Lieutenant, and William Camp was appointed Orderly Sergeant. William Broe, who was wounded at the Battle of Stone River, rejoined us. Captain Standart was acting as Chief of Artillery for the division, and also sitting on the Court Martial board. We received a number of fresh horses from Nashville, together with a lot of new clothing. Several of the members who had been left in hospital at Murfreesboro, returned to duty. We remained in this camp just thirty-eight days.

At 3 o'clock on the morning of Sunday, August 16th, we were all aroused from a sound sleep, with the order to "turn out," and "get ready to march."

This was rather unexpected, and caused considerable surprise, as it was understood that no movement would be made until Monday. But, "*no man knoweth what a day may bring forth.*" So move it was, and at 8 o'clock we were "marching along." About 10 o'clock we crossed Taylor creek, and headed towards McMinnville; but when we had proceeded some five or six miles it clouded up suddenly, and soon we were experiencing one of those thunder storms so peculiar to this region. In a couple of hours the storm had passed over, and the remainder of the day was quite pleasant. We reached Viola near sundown, and camped in a large field near the place.

At daylight all were up and had breakfast, expecting the usual early move. The morning was foggy, but at 8 o'clock the mist cleared away, and two hours later we were on the road.

We now turned off to the right, crossing a small creek; and, as we were now off the McMinnville Pike, our expectations of going to that place vanished. We were once more nonplussed as to what was really our destination. As usual, various opinions were expressed.

It would really be laughable to an outsider to hear the surmises and "yarns" of the men about this, that and the other. One thing, however, was quite evident: that from the direction we were taking, we would soon be among the Cumberland mountains; and it further looked as if we were heading towards Chattanooga.

We soon found ourselves on a road over which we had marched nearly a year previous, and which leads from McMinnville to Altamont. This road is a succession of twists and turns, being similar to a street in Boston: it had no apparent beginning, nor ending.

After a tedious day of it—meeting with some slight accidents—at night we came near a large female seminary, and camped in the woods close by, and two miles from Collins River.

Started at 8 o'clock the next morning, and soon thereafter crossed Collins River. The road was now ascending, being in many places quite steep, and it was with much difficulty that we were enabled to transport our heavy guns. The horses were all pretty well used up at the end of the day, and some of them had given out entirely.

On Wednesday morning, according to orders of the previous evening, we got an early start, and at five o'clock were all on the road. The horses were suffering for want of food, as we had no forage for them, and we were obliged to send them back on the road for a supply.

The road now lay through a thinly settled part of the country, and very rocky and uneven. Water was scarcely to be obtained, and for the want of which there was much suffering. Frequent halts were found necessary, to rest both men and horses. At 2 o'clock we had made about fifteen miles; had now gained the summit, and were about to descend the mountain. We found this part of the road more heavy than that of the morning. In going down a steep pitch, the reach of the forge was broken, and a little further on, two caissons broke down. The men belonging to the detachments, together with the wagon maker, were left with them to make repairs. The remainder of the battery continued on, and at 5 o'clock reached the small town of Dunlap, which is located in Sequatchie Valley, and one mile from the foot of the mountain.

At 10 o'clock on the morning of September 3rd, we once more made a move, and about noon passed through the town of Jasper, making but a short halt. Five miles beyond the town, we crossed the Sequatchie River, and halted on its banks long enough to get dinner. At 4 o'clock we again moved forward, and continued on till about 8 o'clock in the evening, when we halted in a large field, about one mile from the Tennessee River.

Our orders were to unharness horses, but to be prepared to cross the river as soon as the moon rose. Accordingly none ventured to sleep; but we built large fires, cooked supper, and patiently awaited for the moon's rising.

At 10 o'clock Miss Luna showed her face, which was the signal to move; and in a few moments we were on the way to the river. In a short time we reached its bank, and at once commenced crossing by means of ferry-boats; but it was daylight ere all were safely crossed, and at Shellmond.

Shellmond is nothing more than a railroad station, there being only the depot building to give it the name of a place. It is located on the Nashville and Chattanooga railroad, twenty-two miles from Chattanooga, and about sixteen from Stevenson, being on the South bank of Tennessee River. The place had been occupied by the rebels a short time previous to our arrival, but they had been driven out by Union troops. The depot building, which is of brick, showed rough usage from the effects of cannon balls, shell and bullets—it being pretty well riddled.

About one mile from the depot is a large cavern, called the Knick-a-Jack Cave. Nearby, are the salt works, which had been worked by the rebels, but which were mostly destroyed by our troops, at the time the rebels were driven out.

We remained in the above camp until the afternoon of September 5th, when, at 2 o'clock, we were once more on the move.

During our stay here, a large number of troops arrived from different points; and it was now plainly evident that our destination was Chattanooga, or its immediate vicinity, and all were in expectation of soon being once more engaged in deadly array with the enemy. The weather was extremely warm and sultry.

The division to which our battery was attached, proceeded on the direct road to Chattanooga. In many places the road was narrow and rocky, and our progress was necessarily slow. The Tennessee River was frequently in plain view, and the road ran in close proximity to the railroad. We occasionally passed places where the rebels had made a halt, and had hastily erected breastworks, or slight stockades, no doubt from fear of an attack from our forces.

At dark, all were anxiously awaiting for the order to encamp; but in this were disappointed, for we were still kept on the move. At half-past 9 o'clock we passed the ruins of the railroad bridge at Falling Waters. This bridge was formerly a splendid structure, but was now a complete wreck, having been destroyed by the rebels. Three miles further, much to our gratification, we filed into a cornfield and camped for the night.

All were weary and well nigh worn out by the protracted march; but fires were soon lighted, and preparations made for supper.

It so happened that there was—to elegantly describe it—a hog pen nearby, in which were several fine young "porkers," and the men—though contrary to orders—were determined to make an inspection of the place. But how to manage the thing, without alarming the guard, was the question. Finally a plan was arranged: Two of the men were to stand sentry, while one, with axe in hand, and another with keen, glittering blade, were to knock on the head, and cut porkers' throats. This done, they would be thrown out to the sentries, when they would at once drag them off into the field, where the initiated were to be lying in wait to receive them. But, alas! how often are poor mortals' calculations vain. Owing to some blunder, the pigs took the alarm, and beat a hasty retreat into one corner of the pen, and their outcries soon brought a major to the scene of action, who at once arrested all those who were in the vicinity of the pen, and all of whom were innocent of any crime. But to the guard-house they were marched, there to dream of pork in all its forms.

At daylight we were again on the move, and shortly after crossed the Georgia line, being the first time we had ever been in that State.

In many places there were evidences of a grand "skedaddle" having been made by the rebels. The men now anxiously began to enquire along the road the distance to Chattanooga, and what about the enemy. To these questions they received about as intelligent answers as they might expect from a freshly imported Dutchman's "*Nix-cum-erouse*," as all we could learn was, that it was a "right smart distance," and that Bragg had a "heap" of men, and us yankees would wish ourselves "done gone."

At noon, we arrived at Rock Cove Mountain, and, on climbing to its summit, went into camp.

We remained here undisturbed during the following day, when, at evening roll-call, we were ordered to prepare to march. A large number of troops had come in during the day, and it was evident to all that something important was soon to occur.

At 1 o'clock on the morning of September 8th, we resumed our march, and without an incident, at night camped by the roadside. At daybreak the following morning, again moved forward, and just before noon arrived at the celebrated Lookout Mountain, and at once commenced its ascent. We were soon in plain view of Chattanooga; and from the top of this mountain the prospect of the surrounding country was grand and picturesque in the extreme.

Owing to the breaking down of a number of the transportation wagons, it was late in the day ere we were all safely over. But great was our surprise, on now finding ourselves faced in a contrary direction to Chattanooga. Soon, however, we learned that the enemy had evacuated the town, and were retreating towards Lafayette; so in that direction we shaped our course. Proceeding five miles further, we camped for the night.

The next day we continued the march, and now began to have skirmishes with the enemy's rear-guard, and it was thought that a general engagement would soon be brought about.

Shortly before dark, we crossed the small river of Chickamauga, and two miles further on came to a halt.

We moved on the next morning, and after proceeding five miles, halted for dinner. But while we were quietly partaking of our food, a sudden and unexpected assault was made by a force of the enemy's cavalry, which resulted in the capture of about fifty men of the First Kentucky Infantry, of our brigade, and who were on picket guard. So emboldened were the rebels by their exploit, that they made a second dash, and into our very midst. But they met with a sudden check, and were soon put to flight, leaving several of their number dead and wounded in our hands. For the remainder of the day we were not disturbed, and lay in camp till the next morning.

The next day, at 10 o'clock in the morning, we arrived at the small town of Graysville. At this place were several mills and factories, which had been used in manufacturing various articles for the Confederates. These works were ordered to be destroyed, which was speedily accomplished, and soon thereafter we were again moving.

At 2 o'clock p. m., we reached the town of Ringgold. It was near this place that Colonel Creighton, and Lieutenant-Colonel Crane, of the gallant Seventh Ohio Infantry, were soon afterwards killed, while charging up the steeps at the head of their men.

We were here informed that the enemy's rear guard had been

driven from the town by our advance cavalry.

Remaining here for the night, early in the morning we moved forward; but not until we had destroyed the property of the rampant rebels who resided in the place.

Passing through the town, we took a south-easterly course, and soon crossed Chickamauga River. After proceeding about eight miles, our column was suddenly brought to a halt, by our scouts coming in contact with the enemy's rear guard. A lively skirmish now ensued, which resulted to our advantage, as several of the rebels were killed and captured.

After this incident, we continued on our way, and at dark camped near Lee and Gordon's Mills, which are situated on the Chickamauga River. Troops were constantly coming in, and there seemed to be a general concentration of our forces at this point. Something momentous was on the tapis.

Long ere daylight the following morning, we had made preparations to move, and were awaiting orders. From various movements going on in camp, it was apparent that the enemy were meditating mischief, as it was well known that they were in strong force in our immediate vicinity. About dark we changed our position by crossing the river.

At early dawn the next morning all were ready for orders. After waiting for some hours, word reached us that the enemy were retreating. Immediately we were pushed forward, and after going a few miles, arrived at a cross roads, when a halt was ordered.

It was now ascertained that the enemy were gradually falling back to the town of Lafayette, and where it was supposed they would concentrate their force and await an attack.

At 7 o'clock of the same evening, the clear, ringing notes of the bugle summoned us to our respective posts, and in less than ten minutes thereafter we were moving. But instead of going forward, a retrograde movement was made; or, in other words, we fell back. Here was mystery on mystery, to us soldiers, and many a sly wink, or ominous shake of the head, was exchanged. Two days later, however, plainly showed what this movement meant. All along the road flashed the camp-fires of the Union army. The night was cold and cheerless, and around the fires groups of weary, worn-out soldiers were gathered. Many a draft was made on some Confederate's rail fence, for fuel to keep the fires going. Onward we slowly moved, sometimes through corn-fields and woods. At 8 o'clock we turned into a large field, and now expected to go into camp. But in this were disappointed, for an hour later we were again ordered to proceed. Near midnight we turned into a cornfield, and, after considerable manoeuvring, were ordered to pitch tents.

At peep-of-day, on the morning of September 18th, the camp was astir. Breakfast was hurried up, horses fed and wa-tered, and soon we were ready to move. Orders were frequently given, and as often countermanded. Horses were harnessed and unharnessed, some half dozen times; but at last we made a go of it. Every few moments a halt was ordered; and thus it went until the day was nearly ended, and little progress had been made.

Shortly before dark we arrived at Gordon's Mills and came to a halt. Considerable cannonading was now heard on our right, and Madame Rumour, with her thousand tongues, was bus-ily circulating all manner of reports throughout the lines. One thing, however, was certain; and that was, matters must soon come to a focus, which the events of the following day will fully demonstrate.

At 8 o'clock, the same evening, our horses were harnessed and hitched to the guns; but hour after hour went by, and no word to move. Troops were constantly filing past our Battery. We huddled around the campfires and patiently awaited for orders. At midnight came the word to "forward," and away we went. But little did we dream of what was in store for us the day fol-lowing, and which resulted so disastrously to the Army of the Cumberland.

CHAPTER 15

The Battle of Chickamauga

FIRST DAY

At 2 o'clock on the morning of the 19th of September, we passed our former camping ground near Lee and Gordon's Mills, and about one mile beyond, came to a halt. The weather was very cold, but fires were not allowed, and everyone was cautioned to remain as quietly as possible—to keep our stations, and be prepared to obey any orders that might be given.

Although the men were weary and nigh worn out, yet they cheerfully obeyed, as all well knew that danger threatened, and it behooved us to be on our guard.

It was well that this caution was taken, for at daylight, the booming of artillery and the rattle of musketry proclaimed that another battle had commenced.

The enemy, in part, were stationed in a piece of woods near the banks of the Chickamauga River, but in a short time they attempted a flank movement, and the lines of both armies were at once changed. At 9 o'clock the engagement became general, and the enemy now made several desperate charges, but were as often repulsed with heavy loss. At 11 o'clock, the battle raged with great fury, but both sides still maintained their ground, and frequently a fierce hand to hand conflict ensued. Charge after charge did the rebels make in heavy body upon our sturdy lines, and as often were they driven back.

Our battery was exposed to a hot and galling fire, but we maintained our position through the entire day, the guns belching forth a continuous sheet of flame. Several of our men were wounded in the engagement, but none were killed. Lieutenant Baldwin still commanded the battery, and here, as well as at Stone river, he displayed great coolness and bravery.

At dark, hostilities ceased, only to be renewed with greater fierceness on the following day.

SECOND DAY

Early in the morning the battle again opened, when both armies for some time kept up a series of manoeuvrings, each endeavouring to gain some advantage in position. The rebels having greatly superior numbers, were enabled to extend their lines, so that our army was in imminent danger of being outflanked; and at one time they had nearly succeeded in cutting off our communication with Chattanooga. But General Rosencrans had anticipated this, and had made preparations to check the movement, which was successfully done, but not without great loss.

General Bragg, finding himself foiled in this attempt, now ordered a general assault along the entire line, and soon the battle raged with increasing fury.

About this time, a large body of the enemy charged upon our battery. On, on they came, with steady front, feeling confident of victory. But our gallant men wavered not. Nobly did they face their hated foe, and anxiously watched the countenance of our brave captain. Soon he gave the word, and instantly the brazen throats of all our guns spoke out their thunder, and the enemy went down like grass before the scythe. But onward came the foe, and at each instant our guns mowed great gaps in their ranks. Now they were seen to waver—to sway backwards and forwards, and finally when it seemed as if they must surely accomplish their object, they fell back in confusion.

Soon thereafter, a large body of the enemy were massed and thrown forward on our brigade. For a time this assault was withstood, but owing to their superior numbers, the brigade was finally compelled to give way.

The ground over which we retired was very rocky, and covered with a heavy growth of underbrush. Two of our guns had been disabled, by the breaking of the trails. As the enemy were closely pressing us, we were compelled to abandon these guns, which fell into their hands.

During the above charge, several of our company were wounded and taken prisoners.

The retreat now became general, the Union forces slowly retiring towards Chattanooga.

Thus, after nearly two days' hard fighting against a greatly superior force, the Army of the Cumberland were compelled to give up the field.

The Union loss in this engagement was, two thousand and eight hundred killed, eleven thousand and five hundred wounded, and five thousand prisoners. The rebel loss was, from their own account, twenty thousand killed, wounded and prisoners.

Our battery reached Chattanooga about dark the same night, and early the following morning the forge and baggage wagons crossed the river. The army took position in the town and extended their works for several miles along the river. Skirmishing frequently ensued, and the battles of Lookout Mountain, Mission Ridge and Chattanooga were fought, when Bragg was compelled to give up the offensive, and retire, with his whole army, into Georgia.

Conclusion

During the intervals of these battles, our company, as well as the entire Army of the Cumberland, suffered greatly for the want of suitable food. For many days we were on quarter rations; and, for some time, had but one biscuit per day. The horses fared still worse; and it often happened that, for two or three consecutive days, we had nothing wherewith to feed them. The rebels had possession of the country in our front, where forage only could be obtained. They also had command of the Nashville and Chattanooga Railroad, on the South side of the Tennessee River; so, our supplies were transported by wagons by the way of Stevenson.

Finally, it being found impossible to procure provisions for the entire army, a number of batteries were placed in the Reserve Corps. Our battery was of the number.

On the morning of October 19th, the order was given to send all the horses belonging to the Reserve to Stevenson, and that the batteries be moved across the river. This was done, and we went into quarters at Black Oak Ridge, where we found comfortable log houses which had been erected by Union troops, who had previously occupied the place.

We remained in camp at this place, until the Battle of Chattanooga, when, by orders of General Thomas, we were sent to Nashville. Captain Standart had sent in his resignation, which was accepted, and, on the 12th of November, he left for home. The command of the battery now devolved on Lieutenant Baldwin, he being the senior officer on duty.

On Sunday evening, December 6th, we arrived at Nashville, and on the following day went into camp one mile from the city. Five other Batteries occupied the same quarters—all under the personal command of Colonel Barnett. We were designated as the First Division of reserve artillery.

Soon after arriving here, Lieutenant Baldwin—much to the gratification of all the members of the company—received his commission as Captain.

As we now had neither horses nor guns, we led a very easy life of it. Whenever the weather was pleasant, we engaged in outdoor sports—such as ball playing, pitching quoits, etc. But when, as was often the case, the weather was stormy, the time was passed in our tents, reading, writing, and "spinning yarns."

At last, the subject of re-enlisting was broached; but, at first, this did not meet with much favour. Finally, on talking over the matter, and on learning the benefits to be derived from such a course, a few of the men stepped forward and placed their names on the roll. Soon, others did the same, and, by the 4th of January, sixty-five of the old, original members of the company, had re-entered as veterans.

On the 18th of the same month, the veterans were duly mustered in for their new term of service; and a few days later received their back pay, and also their bounty.

The 3rd day of February was a joyful day to us who had re-enlisted; for, on that day we were given the order to return home for a month's furlough.

At 3 o'clock, on the morning of the day following the reception of this order, the bugle was sounded, as a signal for the veterans to form in line. Never did its notes sound sweeter. The roll was called, and all responded to their names but one poor fellow, who had been taken sick, and was in the hospital. The men who had not re-enlisted gave us three rousing cheers, followed by a "tiger," to which we heartily responded. Soon we were on the road to the depot with nimble steps and light hearts; for we were not going to battle, or on one of our long and weary marches. We were "homeward bound."

A half hour later, we were speeding it towards our northern homes. All our past trials and privations were forgotten.

At 9 o'clock on the evening of February, 6th, 1864, we arrived at Cleveland, having been in the service nearly two and a half years.

Appendix

William E. Standart,	Captain.
John A. Bennett,	First Lieutenant.
J. Hale Sypher,	" "
Norman A. Baldwin,	Second "
Eben P. Sturges,	" "
Geo. D. Eldridge,	Quartermaster's Sergeant.
Thos. J. Thompson,	Ordnance "
John J. Kelly,	First "
David H. Throup,	Second "
John H. Blair,	" "
Elisha D. Parker,	" "
Henry Moats,	" "
William M. Camp,	" "
George Wolf,	" "
Wm. Lewhellen,	" "
Alonzo B. Adams,	Corporal.
Alonzo Starr,	"
Edmond A. Nichols,	"
Addison J. Blanchard,	"
Silas H. Judson,	"
Harvey P. Fenn,	"
Joseph G. Lankester,	"
Gerhert Schmidt,	"
Merwin Blanchard,	"
Lewis R. Penfield,	"

Barney McNani,	"
William T. Quilliams,	"
James Willis,	Bugler.
Charles E. Humm,	"
George Luster,	Artificer.
George Schmehl,	"
William C. Hodge,	"
John S. Coleman,	"
William Naylor,	Wagon Master.

Privates.

Jeremiah Arndt,
John Q. Adams,
Joseph Axford,
Robert F. Andrews,
Joseph Binehurer,
David K. Bailey,
John L. Barnes,
Jerome Boice,
James Baker,
Thomas K. Bayard,
John Boon,
Jacob Bluim,
Charles Bull,
Hugh Chambers,
John Elliott,
Samuel Earl,
James H. Fast,
Charles E. Fowler,
Louis Fahrion,
Martin P. Findley,
Charles Furst,
Theodore Gott,
John Grant,
Ransom E. Gillett,
Milo H. Gage,
Thomas M. Hunter,

John G. Courser,
William H. Chapman,
Samuel B. Cole,
Francis Carter,
Newton Crittenden,
William B. Carvey,
Edmond Chapman,
Orlando P. Cutter,
John Dunlap,
Marvin Dodge,
James Disbrow,
Edmond Demilt,
Joseph A. Day,
John David,
Angus McDonald,
George Mason,
James McIlhaney,
John McKinty,
C. C. McIlrath,
Henry McCowan,
Peter Manning,
William McFarland,
Hugh B. Mooney,
William Newcomb,
George Overy,
Edgar M. Peet,

Lewis Hickok,
Percival Holcomb,
Egbert Holcomb,
Byron Hougland,
William R. Hoadley,
Rodman Hart,
Dwight N. Hamlin,
Andrew H. Ives,
John Jackson,
Joshua B. Kerebs,
Lowman Keredzon,
Buchan Kirk,
John Lepper,
William Leary,
Alonzo D. Lee,
Chauncey Lyons,
Charles H. Millis,
A. J. McLaughlin,
Nicholas Schroh,
Adam Sprinkle,
Francis D. Storey,
William H. Singer,
Walter Starr,
John Snyder,
S. W. Shankland,
William R. Stanfield,
Frank H. Seidel,
James N. Sloan,
Benjamin H. Sarles,
Francillion Tanney,
Lewis M. Tyson,
Henry Tyson,
William Twerrell,

Harlan P. Penfield,
Aldin B. Peet,
Royal E. Pease,
George W. Payson,
John W. Pickersgill,
Thomas C. Potter,
James Rosborough,
Frank G. Recklee,
John Ripperton,
George Reading,
Samuel B. Ruple,
Lyman C. Richmond,
John Renouard,
Martin V. B. Richards,
Stephen D. Renouard,
Alexander Stratton,
Erastus H. Stroup,
John Shukers,
Austin VanHaun,
Cyrus B. Vallentine,
Richard Williams,
Wesley Wilson,
Jacob Wolf,
Alonzo White,
Theodore White,
James Webster,
Arthur West,
George Walters,
Daniel White,
Samuel P. Wilson,
John Wellsted,
Frank M. Yeckley.

Privates.

Robert S. Avery,
Charles Abbott,
William Abbott,
David Burnham,
William Broa,
John P. Beers,
John Blanchard,
Orlando D. Cole,
Edwin Chester,
Frank Deidirich,
Walter Dalgleish,
William Freeman,
Balthaser Fischer,
Alfred French,
John French,
William Grant,
G. L. Goodyear,
Silas A. Gardner,
Charles G. Guilford,
Robert S. Graham,
William C. Howe,
Thomas J. Holcomb,
Charles L. Hayden,
T. J. Hudson,
James Hathaway,
Augustus B. Hayes,
Samuel T. Hoyt,
Albert Hawkins,
James S. Jennings,
Conrad Koch,
Patrick Kelley,
Henry Long,
William R. Leonard,

Henry Mace,
Moses Marx,
George Nagle,
H. Olrock,
Fletcher S. Penfield,
Philo A. Penfield,
Henry A. C. Ross,
Charles B. Radder,
Lester J. Richmond,
A. E. Sheldon,
Leonard G. Starr,
Edward E. Swift,
Levi L. Sawtell,
George Smith,
Bradford Teachout,
John Carroll,
Reason B. Case,
Frederick Flick,
F. E. Freeman,
Thomas J. Gill,
John H. Gause,
Alexander Manary,
Dennis Troy,
J. McDonald,
George Wilson,
Thomas Marx,
Harman H. Alms,
Alfred Burton,
Frank Bowers,
Albert Fahrion,
Fayette Green,
Charles Heller,
Richard Miller,

Cuyler Morris,   Eli Wright.

LIST OF MEMBERS OF THE BATTERY WHO WERE KILLED IN BATTLE, OR DIED FROM DISEASE.

George Wolf, First Sergeant,   Killed in Battle.
Chauncey Lyons, Private,   "   "   "
Samuel B. Ruple,   "   "   "
John Elliott,   "   "   "
T. J. Thompson, 1st Serg't, from wounds in Battle.
Thomas C. Potter, Private,   "   "   "   "
T. J. Hudson,   "   "   "   "
John David, Corporal,   "   "   "   "
G. Wilson, Private,   "   "   "   "
John W. Pickersgill, Private,   Killed by Cars.
A. Starr, Corporal,   Died.
D. K. Bailey, Private,   "
W. C. Hodge,   "
E. Chapman,   "
T. White,   "
H. P. Fenn, Corporal,   "
R. Williams, Private,   "
F. Tanney,   "
J. P. Wilson,   "
W. B. Carvey,   "
J. Baker,   "
L. Starr,   "
G. Smith,   "
G. D. Eldridge, Quartermaster's Sergeant,   "
J. P. Beers, Private,   "
A. H. Ives,   "

A Battery at Close Quarters

Henry M. Neil

Contents

The Story of the Eleventh Ohio Battery at Iuka and Corinth

During the Civil War artillery projectiles were divided as to structure into *solid, hollow* and *case shot.* The solid shot were intended to batter down walls or heavy obstructions. Hollow projectiles, called shell and shrapnel, were for use against animate objects; to set fire to buildings and destroy lighter obstructions. Under the head of case shot we had grape and canister. Grape shot is no longer used; being superseded by the machine gun. Canister is simply a sheet iron case filled with bullets and is effective only at very short ranges.

The foremost European military writer, Hohenloe, states that in the Franco-Prussian war, the batteries of the Prussian Guard expended about twenty-five thousand shells and one canister, and that this one canister was broken in transport.

In the official reports of the recent Russo-Japanese War we find that the Arisaka gun, which was the Japanese field piece, has a range of 6,600 meters. The Russian field pieces were said to give good results at 8,000 meters, or five miles. The Japanese, and later the Russians, made a great feature of indirect fire. Having located a mass of the enemy, probably beyond two ranges of hills, they would stake out a line indicating the direction, then secure the range by the use of shells which gave out a yellowish vapour on bursting. This vapour being observed and signalled by scouts also indicated the necessary angles of departure from the line of stakes and enabled the artillerymen, miles away from actual contact, to complacently try experiments in battle ballistics with very little fear of being interrupted by an enemy.

The range of modern field artillery being officially reported at five miles, permit me to take you back to a day, over forty-seven years ago, when an Ohio battery, placed in the extreme front of battle, fought at less than fifty yards.

The village of Iuka lies in the northeast corner of the State of Mississippi. The neighbouring country is broken and, in 1862, was covered with forests. Northwesterly from Iuka lies the village of Burnsville and further on the little city of Corinth, close to the Tennessee line. In 1862 Corinth possessed strategical advantages which caused it to become a large supply depot for the Federal armies. South of Corinth and southwest of Iuka, the town of Jacinto was located.

On the eighteenth of September, 1862, General Sterling Price lay at Iuka with an army of about twenty thousand Confederates. General E. O. G. Ord's force lay between Burnsville and Corinth and had just been reinforced by Ross's division. Burnsville was seven miles from Iuka. General Rosecrans lay at Jacinto, nineteen and one-half miles from Iuka.

General Grant, taking advantage of this situation, ordered a combined attack by Ord and Rosecrans upon General Price. Under this order Rosecrans moved from Jacinto at 3:00 a. m. September 19th, and was within striking distance of Price's patrols by noon. Ord was to attack from the west and draw Price in that direction while Rosecrans was to move to the rebel rear by the Jacinto and Fulton roads and cut off their retreat. Neither of these Union armies was powerful enough to make, alone, a successful attack upon Price.

The strategical plan of attack above outlined was not carried out. Ord's strategy never reached the domain of tactics, for he went into camp seven miles west of Iuka and the head of Rosecrans' column was attacked by the entire army of Price. It was with the head of this column that the Eleventh Ohio Battery marched into the fight. Anticipating a combined engagement the head of the column pushed its innocent way into the maw of the entire rebel army. We had to fight first and think afterward. Price had hours to choose his positions and, incidentally, he chose our position also. We didn't have time to change it.

Rapidity of movement and surprise are the life and soul of the strategical offensive.

That maxim reads well but, in practice, it is important to provide against being surprised by the other fellow before you spring your surprise on him.

For several miles in the afternoon of the 19th of September the advance of Rosecrans' column was warmly contested. The enemy's sharp-shooters occupied every point of vantage, making the last five miles a steady contest. The cavalry had long ago been driven in. A few companies formed an advance skirmish line only a short distance from the main column. Near the front of the column marched the Eleventh Ohio Battery. The men knew that an engagement was imminent but their immediate front was unknown and unexplored. As usual, we had no maps. While marching through a defile at the crest of a thickly wooded hill we noticed that the rifle fire in front was suddenly increased. But there was no pause to reconnoitre. The battery marched from the defile into within short range of Price's whole army. Instantly an entire rebel division concentrated its fire on the battery with the intention of annihilating it before it could unlimber.

As we emerged from the cut this sudden concentration of rifle fire gave me the impression of being in a violent hail storm. Riding at the head of the column I turned my head to look for the men, expecting to see half the men and horses down. To my great joy I found all uninjured. The storm of bullets was passing just over our heads. We hastened to get into position and unlimber before they could get the range. Just in front of us the road turned to the right. We turned to the right into the brush and took position facing this road. As our men were clearing the hazel brush for positions for their guns a Wisconsin battery appeared about three or four hundred yards to our left and unlimbered; but it suddenly limbered up and galloped to the rear without having fired a shot. It had been ordered back, leaving the Eleventh the only Union battery in the battle.

The Fifth Iowa took position just at our right. The Twenty-sixth Missouri prolonged the line to the right of the Fifth Iowa. On our left the Forty-eighth Indiana formed a line that swung somewhat forward at its left flank. Our side of the fight began with these three regiments in position. The front thus hastily formed did not permit of further extension, owing to the nature of the ground.

A little later the Fourth Minnesota and Sixteenth Iowa were, respectively, echeloned in rear of the left and right flanks. The total force actually engaged was 2800 Union and 11,000 Confederates.

When the Eleventh went into position Lieutenant Sears was in command. As junior First Lieutenant, I had the right section, while Second Lieutenant Alger fought the centre section. Of the acting Second Lieutenants Perrine had the left section and Bauer the line of *caissons*. During the fight I succeeded to the command when Sears went to the rear with a wound. Alger was captured. Bauer was killed.

The battery had taken position in line from column under an infantry fire from an entire division at ranges of from 200 to 400 yards. Shells from the rebel artillery were also crashing through our line. We opened fire at first with shell. This shell fire proved so effective that a rebel assault on the battery was ordered. A division of Price's army rushed to the charge. The battery changed from shell to double charges of canister. The effect of the canister was terribly increased because of the rebel method of charging in masses. Had the line to the left of the battery held its front the assault on the battery would have been impossible of success. But Col. Eddy of the 48th Indiana was killed and the survivors of his regiment were swept back by overwhelming numbers. The left flank of the battery was thus left bare and unsupported. On the right the Fifth Iowa was cut to pieces. Only eleven officers and a handful of men remained. With the line melted away the battery found itself facing in three directions and battling with masses on three fronts. It had a rear but no flanks. The guns were being worked with greater speed and smaller crews. Cannoneers were falling. Other cannoneers coolly took their places and performed double duty. Drivers left their dead horses and took the places of dead or wounded comrades, only to be struck down in turn. Of eighty horses only three remained standing and a withdrawal of the guns was impossible. The surviving men were too few to do more than work the guns. Finally the charging hordes, checked and mutilated again and again in front, to right and to left, pressed close. Eight thousand men against two score. On the fifth charge the survivors were finally choked from the guns they would not abandon.

General Rosecrans in his notice, in orders, of the facts and results of the battle of Iuka, states that the Eleventh Ohio Battery participated:

> Under circumstances of danger and exposure such as rarely, perhaps never, have fallen to the lot of one single battery during this war.

In the same order the commanding general further states:

> On a narrow front, intersected by ravines and covered with dense undergrowth, with a single battery, Hamilton's division went into action against the combined rebel hosts. On that unequal ground, which permitted the enemy to outnumber them three to one, they fought a glorious battle, mowing down the rebel hordes until, night closing in, they rested on their arms on the ground, from which the enemy retired during the night, leaving us masters of the field.

General Hamilton's official report, in describing the action of the Union left flank, states:

> Colonel Sanborn, in command of the first brigade, most gallantly held the left in position until, under a desolating carnage of musketry and canister, the brave Eddy was cut down, and his regiment, borne down by five times

their numbers, fell back in some disorder on the Eightieth Ohio, under Lieutenant-Colonel Bartilson. The falling back of the Forty-eighth exposed the battery. As the masses of the enemy advanced the battery opened with canister at short range, mowing down the rebels by scores, until, with every officer killed or wounded and nearly every man and horse killed or disabled, it fell an easy prey. But this success was short lived.

The hero Sullivan rallied a portion of the right wing, and, with a bravery better characterized as audacity, drove the rebels back to cover. Again they rallied and again the battery fell into their hands; but with the wavering fortunes of this desperate fight the battery again fell into our hands, and with three of its guns spiked and the carriages cut and splintered with balls, it is again ready to meet the foe.

At the close of the engagement the ground in front of the battery showed heaps of dead bodies. Statistics show that the Confederates' loss in this engagement amounted to eight hundred in killed and wounded. While actual inspection of the field of carnage indicated that a large proportion of the slain had met their death from the canister of the Eleventh. The Brigade Commander's report states that the battery fired with great rapidity and extraordinary accuracy.

The battery entered the fight with ninety-seven men and five officers, commissioned and acting. Of these, eighteen were killed and thirty-nine wounded, many mortally. A number of the wounded had been bayoneted at their guns. Of the cannoneers alone, forty-six were killed or wounded. Forty-six out of a total of fifty-four. More than five men out of every six.

The statistics compiled by Col. Fox in his *Regimental Losses in the American Civil War*, show that this day's record in killed and mortally wounded equalled, within one, the total killed in any light battery during its entire term of service. This work also states that the losses of the Eleventh at Iuka were 22% greater than those sustained by any other light battery in any one engagement during the war.

You have been familiar with death and wounds and the aching pain of deep sympathy for suffering comrades. Therefore I will not depict the tortures and individual heroisms of those artillerymen who fell, to die or partly recover. Those who died left a legacy of glory and honour to posterity and to their country. That legacy is of greater value than the greatest riches, for it will always endure, and the martyrs of the civil war, the dead and the living, will proudly bear to the throne of God those scars which were the price of their country's salvation.

One singular feature of this fight was that but two members of the battery were taken prisoners. The guns were captured and recaptured several times before dark. The battery men had never abandoned them voluntarily. One Confederate prisoner afterward said:

Those battery boys had so much spunk that we took pity on a few who were left.

It may have been this respect for the courage of the artillerymen which induced the Confederates to let the few survivors go. But could they have looked into the future and seen these same men and guns at Corinth only fourteen days later, they would probably have dropped every other work and secured them while they had this one chance.

After attending to the wounded, the night after the fight at Iuka, all members of the battery were ordered to a rendezvous. They were all assembled by 5 a. m. and, after reverently burying our dead, the men turned their attention to securing the guns and equipments scattered over the field. The drivers cried softly as they removed the harness from their faithful mounts. In one mass lay eighteen dead horses. These three teams, instead of trying to escape, had swung together and died together. My own horse received seven wounds. Toward the close of the engagement he sank down and was left for dead. Sometime during the night he revived and was found by an officer of Rosecrans' staff who rode him until daylight. This horse survived the war two years, then suddenly dropped dead in his stall. A bullet had finally worked its way into an artery.

Of the other three surviving horses one had an interesting history. He was a fine strong bay who always worked as near leader. At our first battle, New Madrid, this horse's rider was literally cut in two by a thirty-two pound ball. The horse kept his place, covered with the blood of poor James Bibby. After this baptism he seemed to bear a charmed life. He was mustered out with the battery, still able to do full duty.

Early in the morning after the battle General Rosecrans ordered me to refit the battery as rapidly as possible. After the guns' spikes were removed the pieces were found to be in serviceable order and work on the splintered carriages was begun.

A description of our six guns may be of interest. They were:

2 rifled 6 pounders, bronze, (James pattern), (calibre 3.67, weight of ball, 14 lbs.)
2 smooth bore 6 pounders, (calibre 3.67, weight of ball, 14 lbs.)
2 twelve pounder Howitzers, (calibre 4.62.)

These guns would soon be needed again, for General Rosecrans had promised us more work in the near future at Corinth. In this emergency I was allowed to draw horses and equipment from the nearest available sources without regular requisition. General Rosecrans' foresight in stretching regulations further permitted me to obtain recruits from my brigade commander, and the rejuvenation of the Eleventh was soon under way. The new men were drilled as hard as their other duties permitted. The battery was ready for the march to Corinth by the evening of October 1st.

General Rosecrans had left orders with Colonel Crocker, who was left in command at Iuka, to furnish the Eleventh with an escort to Corinth. On the evening of October first I found that an escort could not be secured for two or three days, as Colonel Crocker had only enough men present for guard and picket duty.

My orders were to report at Corinth as soon as possible. The news from there indicated that a big battle was imminent. It also indicated that the Eleventh ran some risk of capture if it went through alone. But there was no way to avoid that risk. I therefore drew some extra horses, sent mounted cannoneers forward as an advance guard, and started for Corinth on the morning of October second. I felt very uneasy at starting on that march for I knew that, if I met one of the numerous strong bands of guerrillas or a Confederate force, I might be shot up first and court-martialed afterward.

Nothing unusual happened during the day's march. By four p. m. we were inside our own lines and a little later the battery was assigned to a strange brigade. By the morning of October third I managed to secure an order sending us to our old brigade. It looked much smaller than before Iuka but that made us think all the more of it.

After the failure of his Napoleonic tactics at Iuka, General Price retreated to Ripley, Mississippi, where he united with a still stronger rebel force, under General Van Dorn. Van Dorn assumed command of the united forces and pushed forward toward Corinth with intent to overwhelm Rosecrans.

Corinth was surrounded by extensive works constructed by Beauregard when he held that position against Halleck's army. Rosecrans had too few troops to man these works but had taken the precaution to hastily construct an inner line of fortifications, which was traced about a mile west from the centre of the village.

The cavalry had promptly notified Rosecrans of the formidable rebel movement northward and he had hurriedly prepared to receive it. About 10 a. m. on October third we moved from our camp east of Corinth, marching through the town to a designated point at the right of the Federal lines. These lines occupied the outer line of works built by Beauregard.

At about 2 p. m. we received the order to fall back to the new line, nearer Corinth. In executing this movement I saw several heavy columns of rebels approaching, *en route* with the same objective. It looked for a time as if we might be surrounded, but nothing resulted except a few singing bullets which did no harm. It was evident that the rebels felt that we were in a trap and they were pursuing a prearranged plan in springing it. As we reached the north-western suburb of Corinth we swung to the left and continued until we reached the right wing of the new line, where we selected a fine position on rising ground with a clear field of fire and a magnificent view.

The new defensive line of which we had just formed a part, presented a concave front to Van Dorn's army. Our elevated position enabled the batterymen to see both lines of battle. Being at the Federal right flank we became one of the horns of the dilemma which confronted Van Dorn's hosts the next day.

Van Dorn's magnificent series of assaults against our line began about 9:30 the next morning. The masses of the enemy first attacked our left flank and were repulsed. Then they assailed our centre, penetrated it, but were at length driven back into the cross fire of our artillery.

By 2 p. m. the attacks against the left and centre had exhausted themselves and the peril of a broken centre was narrowly averted. Then the rebels, having concentrated for another supreme effort, bore down upon Hamilton's division on the right. This was good tactics, because our right had been weakened by sending troops to the imperilled centre.

The now familiar sight of masses of rebels, screaming the familiar yell, appeared in our front. As the mass approached I recognized them and called to the men:

Boys, there are the same troops that fought us at Iuka; are you going to let them touch our guns today?

The yell of rage that went up was more ominous than a rebel yell ever tried to be.

At six hundred yards the Eleventh opened with shell. The men worked like tigers in their desperate resolve that their beloved guns would never again feel the insult of a rebel touch.

Three times they charged and three times they were repulsed. Each time they came so close that we resorted to double charges of canister and never a rebel reached the muzzles of our guns. By four o'clock the Confederates were staggering back or surrendering in squads.

From some prisoners taken at Corinth it was learned that they were still unnerved from the moral effect of their assaults at Iuka. Those prisoners stated that, as they went into the assault, they recognized the bark of the guns of the Eleventh Ohio. Before these guns they had seen hundreds of their comrades fall like wheat before the harvester. They felt that they could not again silence the guns of the Eleventh. It had taken five assaults to do so when the odds were many to one.

At daylight of October 5th, after a night spent in convoying prisoners and caring for the wounded, we started in pursuit of the remains of Price's and Van Dorn's armies. During that day's march our army simply gathered in throngs of rebels. The retreating force had been three days without regular rations and were too weak to escape.

For two long days and nights we pressed our foes until our condition was hardly better than theirs. At one a. m. on the second night's march, we were stumbling along, almost dead with fatigue, when suddenly a band struck up the familiar song—*John Brown's Body*. Other bands joined; we all woke up and were soon swinging along without a thought of our condition. I have often wondered what moral effect this musical demonstration, at dead of night, had upon our quarry.

It took us three days to return to Corinth, horses stumbling with weariness, men asleep in their saddles, tired but happy, a victory won against odds.

"An Army Experience"

The following appreciative remembrance of the action of the Eleventh Ohio Battery at Battles of Iuka, September 19, 1862, and Corinth, October 4, 1862, appeared in the columns of the *St. Paul (Minnesota) Pioneer Press* in 1884. Having been preserved by a Companion of the Ohio Commandery, it was read by the recorder, Major Thrall, at the Commandery monthly meeting of October 6, 1909, as the recorder's contribution to the discussion of an account of the part of the Eleventh Ohio in those battles, which had just been presented by Captain Neil, and by general request is published by the Commandery, without the advice or consent of Companion Neil.

Geo. A. Thayer,

A. B. Isham,

L. M. Hosea,

Publication Committee.

No scenes of life are so deeply and indelibly impressed upon the memory as those which occur in war and battle. All the mental faculties seem to be melted into a fused condition by the excitement of the occasion, so that a full and deep impression of all the principal events is made and then to be suddenly turned to adamant so that the impression must remain as long as the faculties endure. There is not a soldier of the late war, who took part in any engagement, who does not have impressed upon his mind some event or scene which then transpired that is just as vivid and fresh today as on the day it was made.

And when the memory is turned toward it by the suggestion of any other faculty—by the sight of some party connected therewith, or hearing kindred sounds, or by those more hidden spiritual influences less understood that at times cause to form in order and pass in review before the mind all the leading and exciting incidents of past life, these events and scenes are again displayed with all the vividness and strength of first impression. These thoughts were suggested to the writer upon meeting Lieutenant H. M. Neil of the Eleventh Ohio Battery at the meeting of the Society of the Army of the Tennessee at St. Louis, in 1882.

Twenty years had passed since I had seen his face, and I had reckoned him among the brave spirits of the war which had gone to rest. When I saw him last before this, he was commanding his battery in the thickest of the fight at the Battle of Corinth about 11 o'clock in the forenoon of October 4, 1862. His rank was that of second lieutenant. All officers of higher grade were absent in hospital from wounds received fifteen days before at Iuka, in which battle this battery of a few more than 100 men had eighteen killed and fifty-two wounded, and out of 148 horses had but three left standing at the close of the engagement. The battery was captured by the rebels and recaptured by our troops. Lieutenant Neil was the only commissioned officer on duty at the close of the engagement, and he had been wounded twice with shell and twice with bullets—severe flesh wounds. He was besmeared with blood.

The lieutenant was, notwithstanding full of pluck. He said the next morning, 'If I can have one hundred men detailed from the infantry and horses furnished, I will have the battery in fighting trim again in two weeks.' Infantry soldiers readily volunteered upon call to man the battery, and horses were furnished by the quartermaster, and on the afternoon of the 3rd of October—fourteen days from the annihilation of the battery the Battle of Corinth was fought and the lieutenant having marched up from Iuka without escort, came upon the field with his battery fully manned, equipped and drilled, amid the hurrahs and tears of the infantry that had seen it destroyed under the terrible fire of the 19th of September, and who now seemed to feel that the battery men, horses and all, had come back from the regions of the dead to aid in the terrible struggle now going on between the same armies.

The lieutenant received the heartiest congratulations of all officers who had been with him in the Battle of Iuka. While receiving those of the writer he said:

> I want you to stay right by my battery with your regiment when it goes into action here, and if you will no rebel battalions can take it this time.

There was a promise to comply with his request. On the following morning when the irresistible assault of the rebel army came, the Eleventh Ohio Battery was in position commanding the whole rebel line and the Fourth Minnesota Infantry in line flat upon the ground close in its rear.

Lieutenant Neil was seated on his thoroughbred from twenty to forty feet in front of the battery, between the line of fire of the guns of the middle section. He requested the colonel of the infantry to keep his eye upon him and whenever he beckoned with his saber, to have the infantry rise up and deliver their fire.

Now the assaulting lines of the rebel armies come on like a wave of the sea, rolling along over breastworks and batteries. He orders the men to open fire and, still in his advanced position, waves his hat constantly to the advancing lines of rebels, and shouts, 'Come on! Come on! if you think you can play Iuka over again.' A strange coincidence was that the same rebel battalions came against this battery that had captured it on the 19th of September. But they could not come on here. Three times the lieutenant signalled the infantry to rise and fire, and each time they rose to hear him say, 'No, no, they have broke again.'

For a half mile in front of this battery, after the battle, were large areas covered with the dead and dying, which told with what terrible effect it had been served during the assault.

The sight of the lieutenant, after twenty years, brought up these occurrences—this whole scene, and made it as fresh as if it had transpired yesterday, and made me resolve to commit it to writing before I died, feeling that none of us had done him justice in our reports of these battles.

The scene at Corinth, if it could be placed on canvas, would be thrilling even to strangers. An elegant thorough-bred Kentucky horse fully caparisoned, on which the lieu-tenant is sitting erectly, with his hat in his hand, is standing out in front of the battery between the lines of fire of the two centre guns, seemingly conscious that if he moved to the right or left he would be torn to atoms, and trusting himself wholly to his rider, the lieutenant is waving his hat in the air, and bidding defiance to the foe; advancing in masses and lines upon his positions, the artillerymen with superhuman power and skill, amid the smoke that rolled incessantly from the muzzles of every gun, loading and firing, is a picture before the mind at this distance plainer than can be placed on canvas by the most skilful artist. It is such men and such services that saved this nation in the war. They were not conspicuous nor vain-glorious, per-haps not heard of before the war, nor afterwards; but in the midst of it, meeting the full demands of the great occasion and leaving the reward to posterity.

What this officer did after this battle in the war, I know not. He passed from my sight when we withdrew from that line of battle, and twenty years passed before I saw his face again, and during all this time never heard a word concerning him. When I met him it was my privilege to name him as one of the vice presidents of our soci-ety, showing that time had in no respect obliterated or dimmed the memory of his services.

John B. Sanborn, Commanding,
First Brigade, Seventh Division,
Army of the Tennessee.
St. Paul, Jan. 14, 1884.